AGELESS INDIA - 3

AGELESS INDIA - 3

APOSTLE OF THE TWENTIETH CENTURY—M.K. GANDHI

Curated by
Kinnari Bhatt and Tridip Suhrud

Series Editor
MALVIKA SINGH

LIMITED
EDITIONS

AN IMPRINT OF
ACADEMIC FOUNDATION

INTRODUCTION TO THE SERIES

This series of Notebooks was conceived as a vibrant and energetic representation of India, manifesting images of her past and present, her remarkable and infinite civilisation with its endless layers of diversity merging and melding into one another, creating a fabric of seamless transitions laced with overlaps of buoyant contradictions that are often unpredictable and mysterious, allowing for flights of the imagination, and leaving 'room for wonder'.

Through the pages of *Ageless India*, this extraordinary and finely nuanced, ever-evolving and contemporary destination on earth, continues to draw into its complex unstitched folds, the many stories and experiences, the influences and ideas that emerge from a 'planet', continually revolving ecliptically on its firm axis, sharing experience and endorsing a sublime unity in exciting and invigorating diversity.

The voyeur in us can use these books to exchange notes, share ideas, articulate intangible reflections in words, and more, to leave them as 'memories' that can be savoured today, as well as in the years to come, by family and friends, to keep the connect of the past with the future alive.

Ageless India will showcase the personalised 'India' of men and women impassioned by her many 'plots' and 'sub-plots', using the skill of their hands and eyes to capture for posterity, her changing avatars, her multiple expressions. The series will be infinite...

Malvika Singh
New Delhi 2015

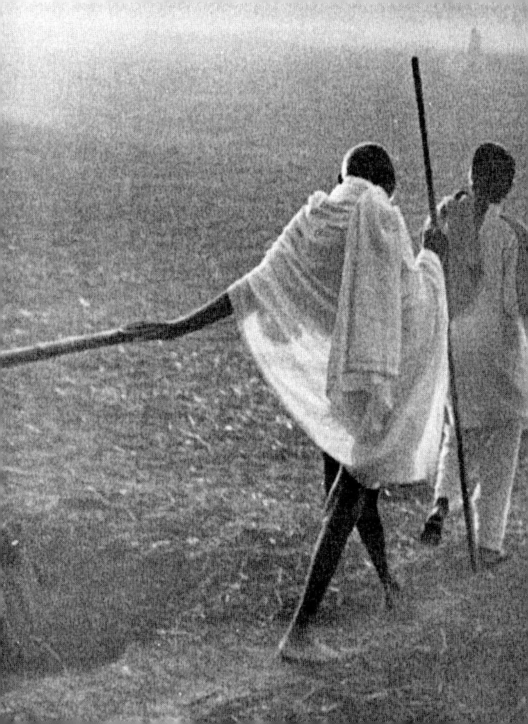

AGELESS INDIA - 3

APOSTLE OF THE TWENTIETH CENTURY—M.K. GANDHI

These rare and iconic images of Mohandas Karamchand Gandhi, the Mahatma who invoked non-violence as the potent weapon of protest in the quest for freedom and liberation of mind and spirit, are selected from the valuable and treasured archives that have been carefully preserved at his ashram at Sabarmati in Gujarat. This compendium of visuals traces the trajectory of a life inspired by a single cause, motivated by unwavering passion. He was a true Mahatma, grounded in the earth of India, fearless and free from human bondage.

Series Editor
MALVIKA SINGH

Cover image (previous page):
Striding on...

Cover image (previous page):
Striding on...

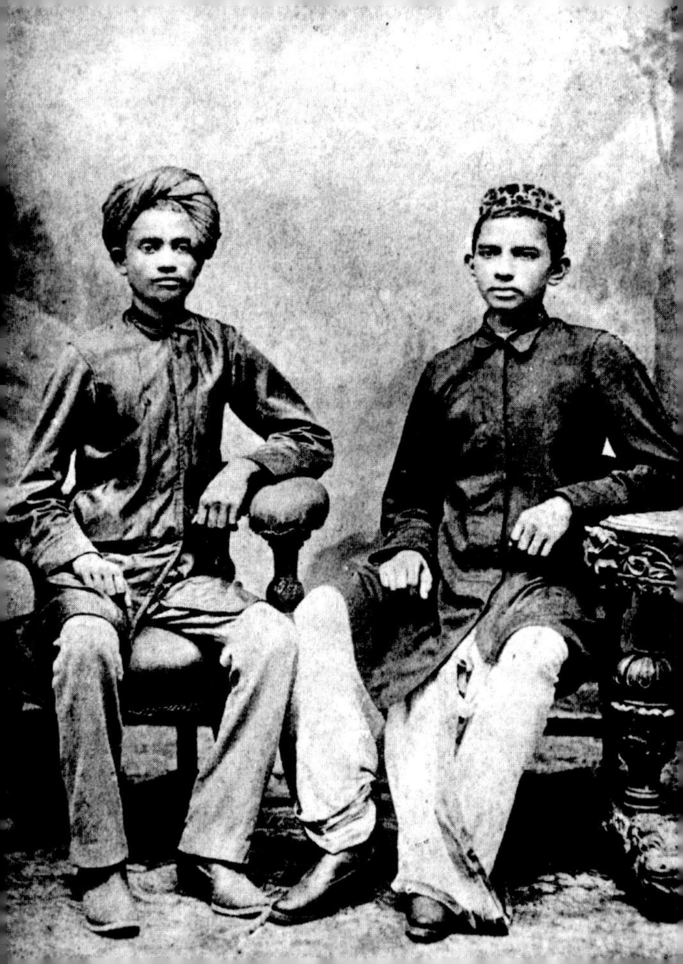

Mohandas Karamchand Gandhi with his school mate, Shaeikh Mehtab.

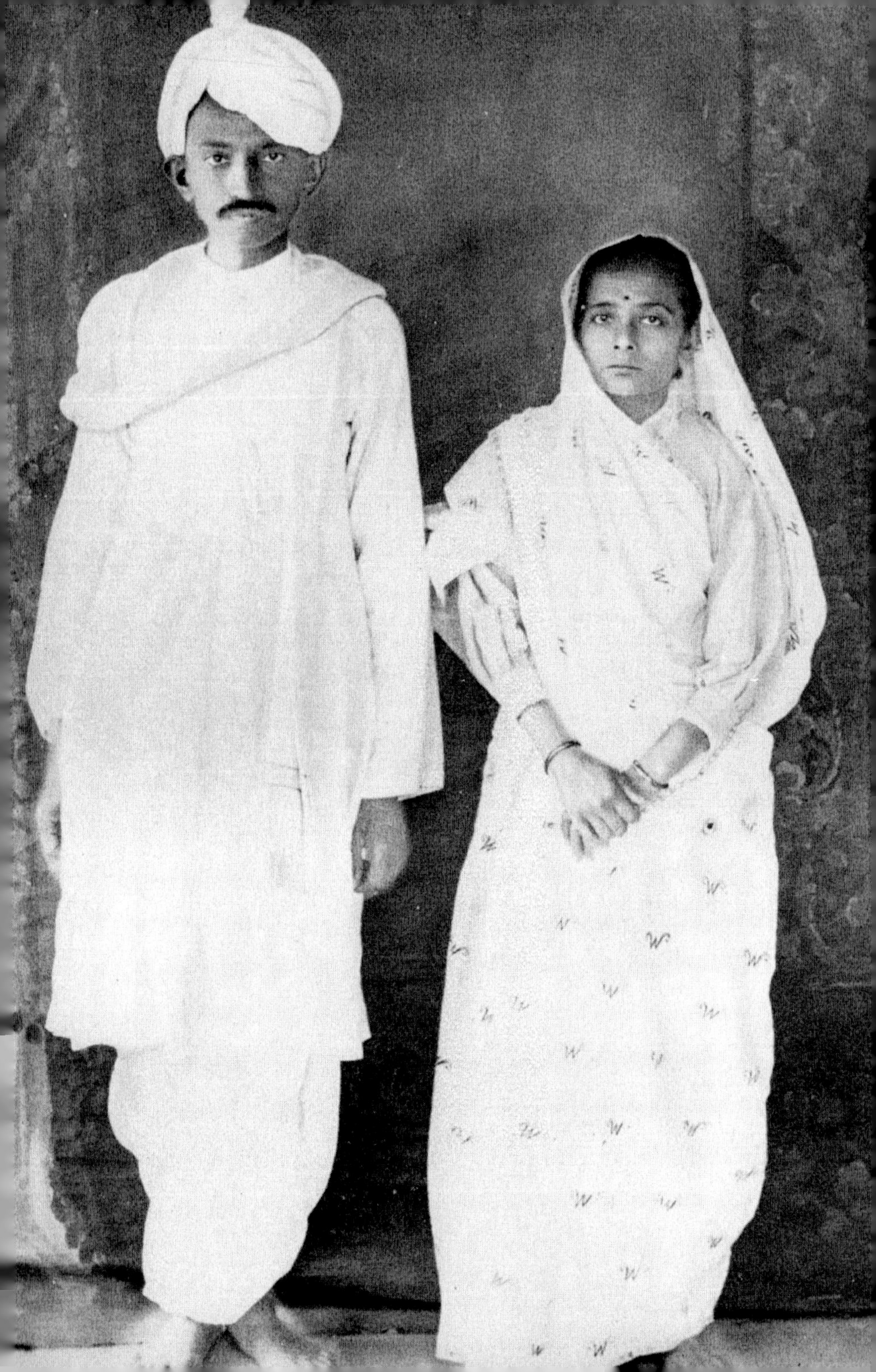

Gandhi and Kasturbai on their return to India, January 1915.

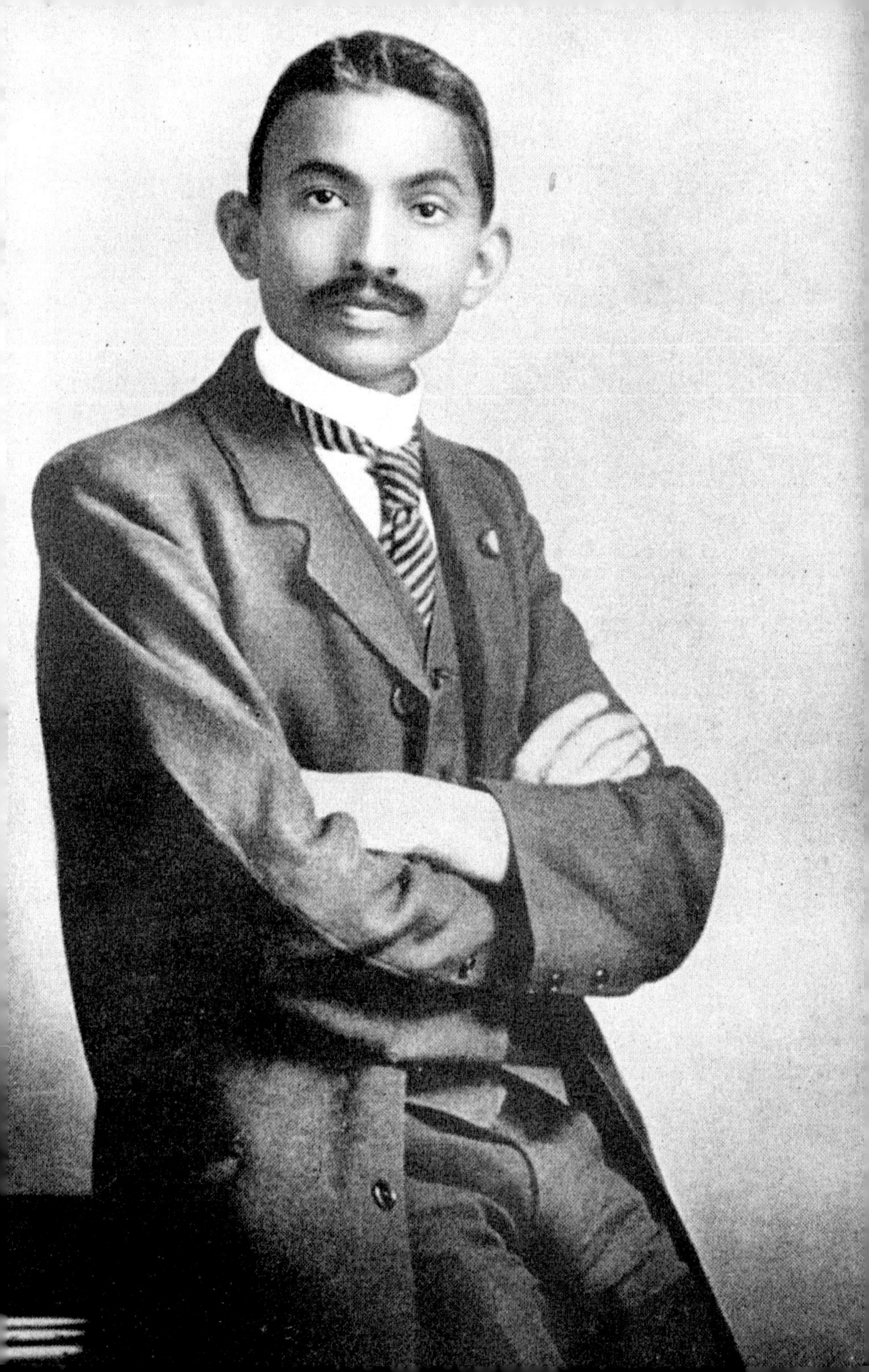

As a barrister wearing the
London Vegetarian Society's badge,
Johannesburg 1906.

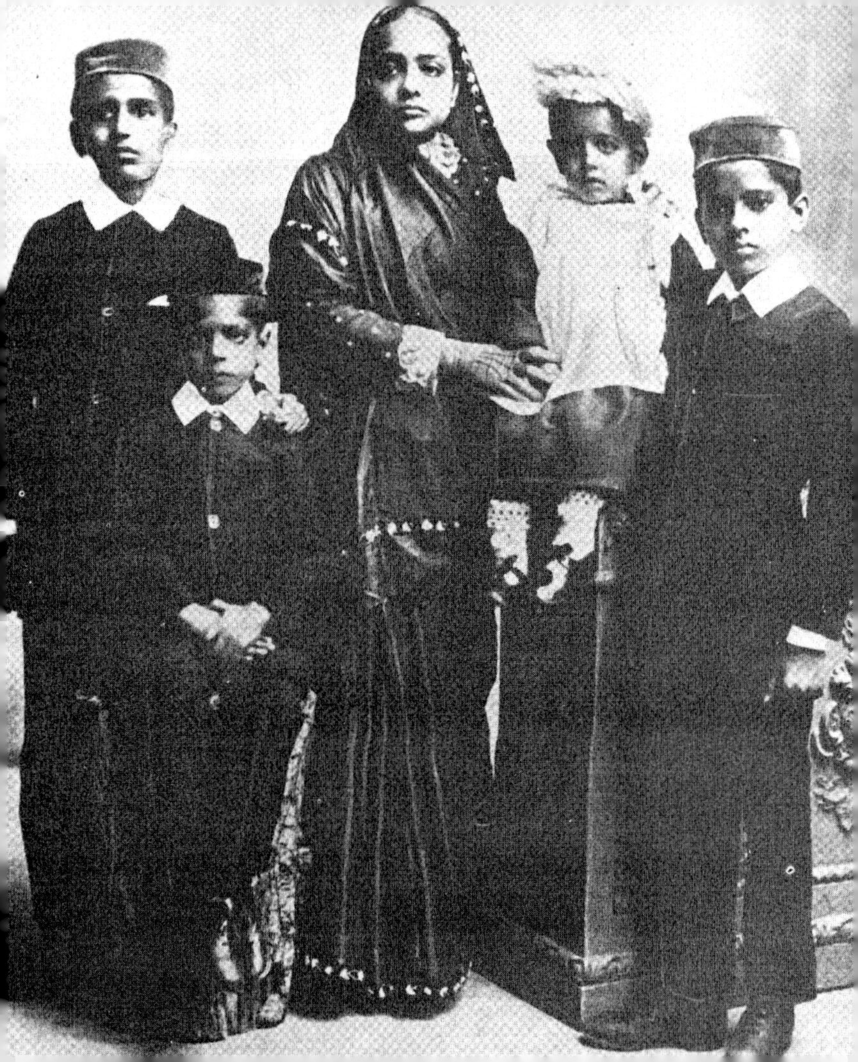

Kasturbai Gandhi with nephew Gokuldas (left), and sons Manilal, Ramdas and Harilal.

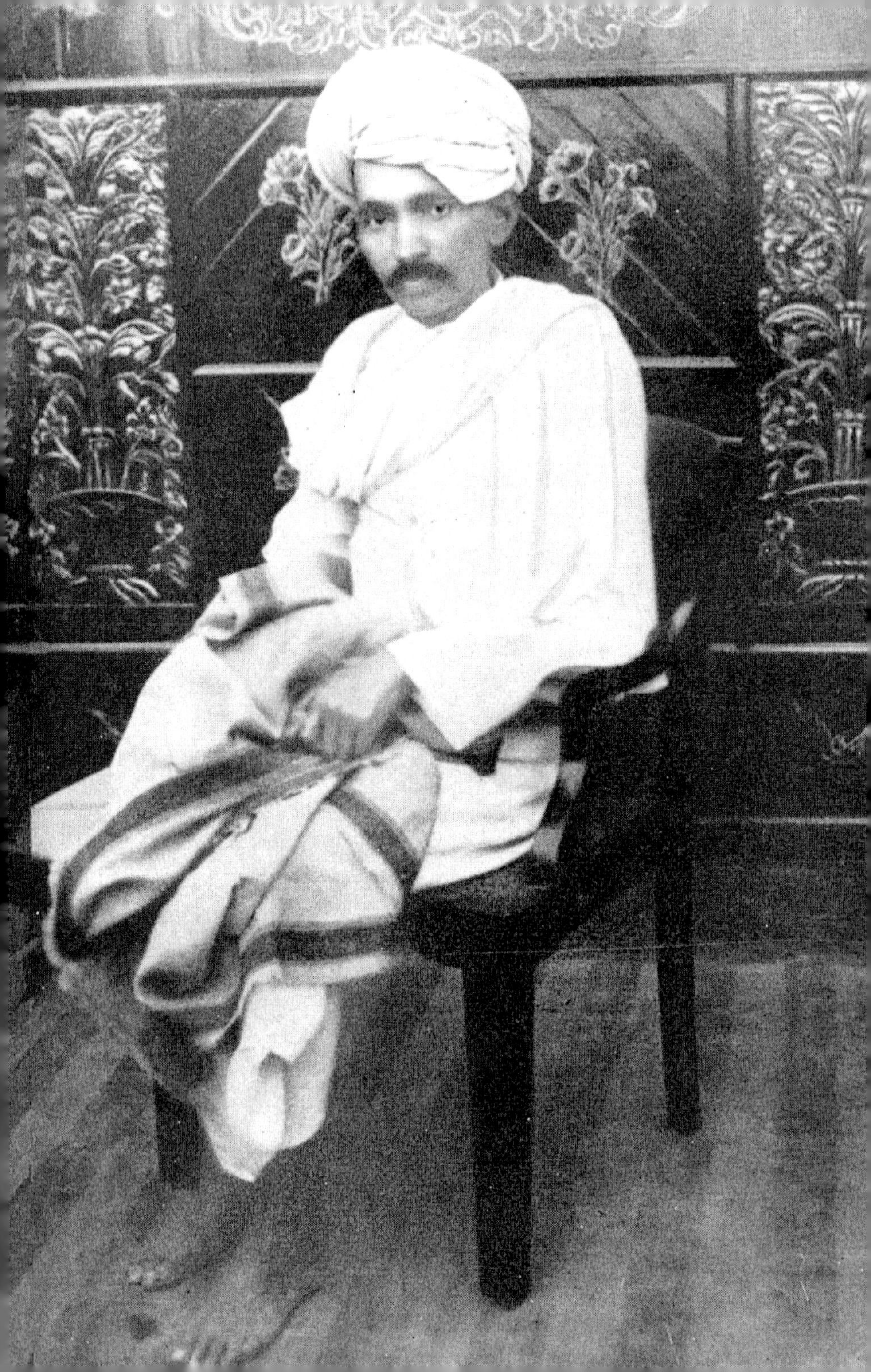

Gandhi during the Kheda Satyagraha, 1918.

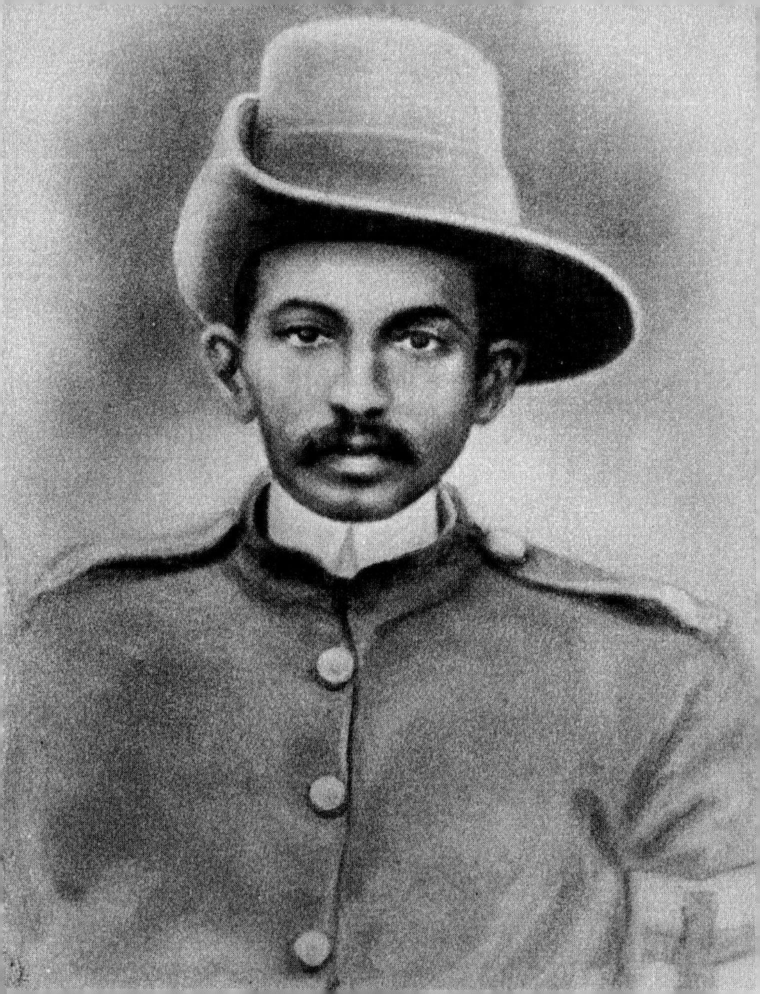

In the uniform of Indian Ambulance Corps.

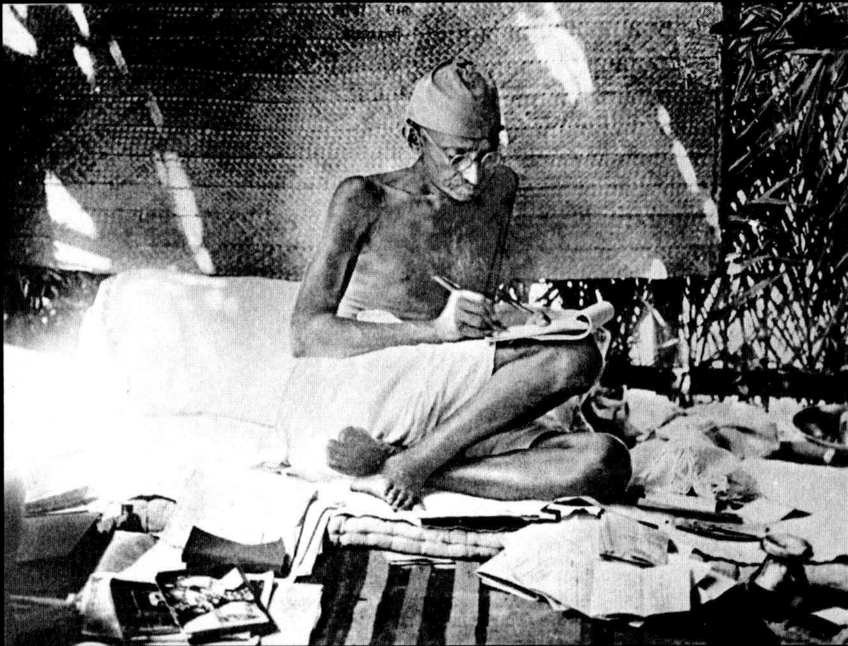

andhi at work, Karadi, May 1930.

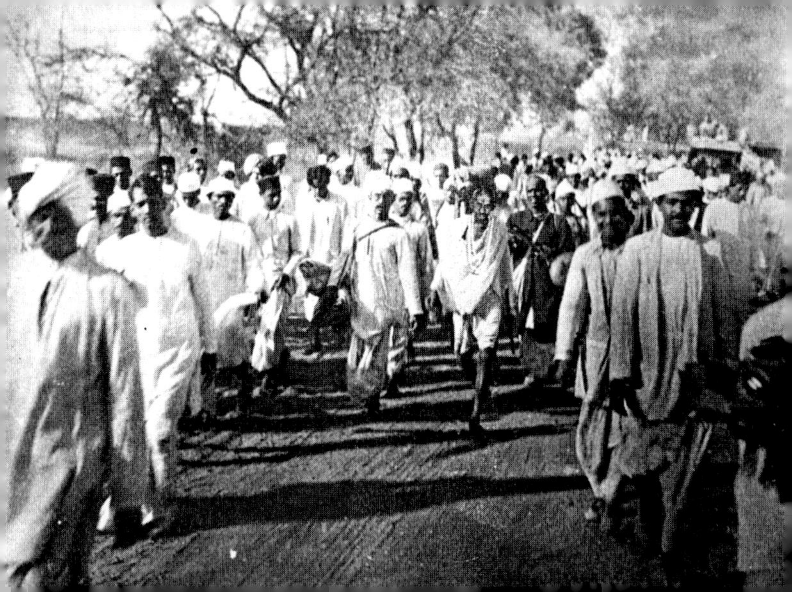

Dandi March in progress.

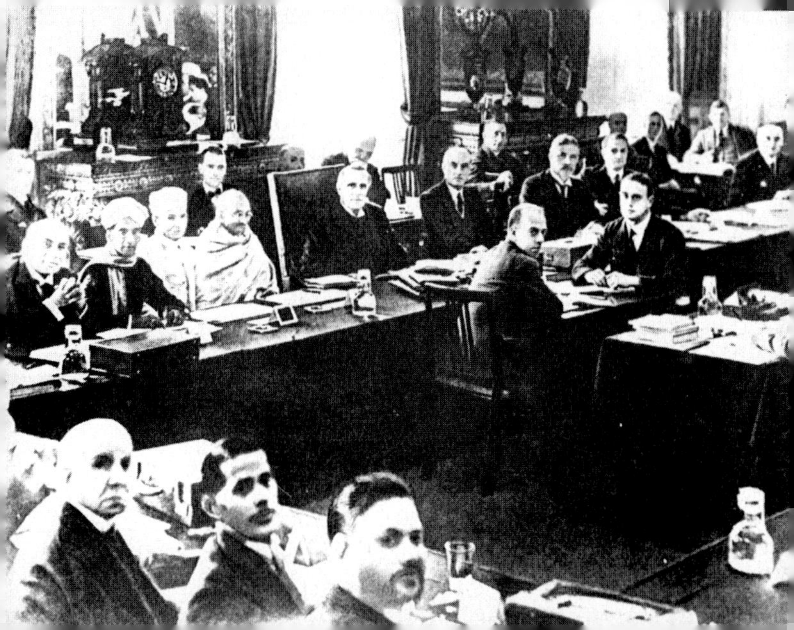

Second Round Table Conference,
London, 1931.

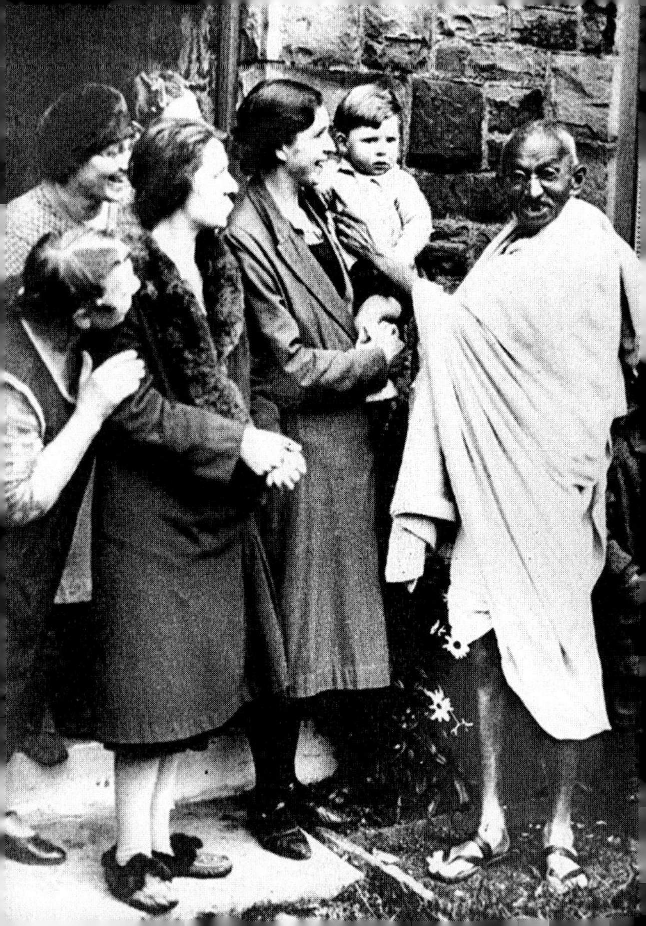

Gandhi with textile workers at Darwen, Lancashire, September 26, 1931.

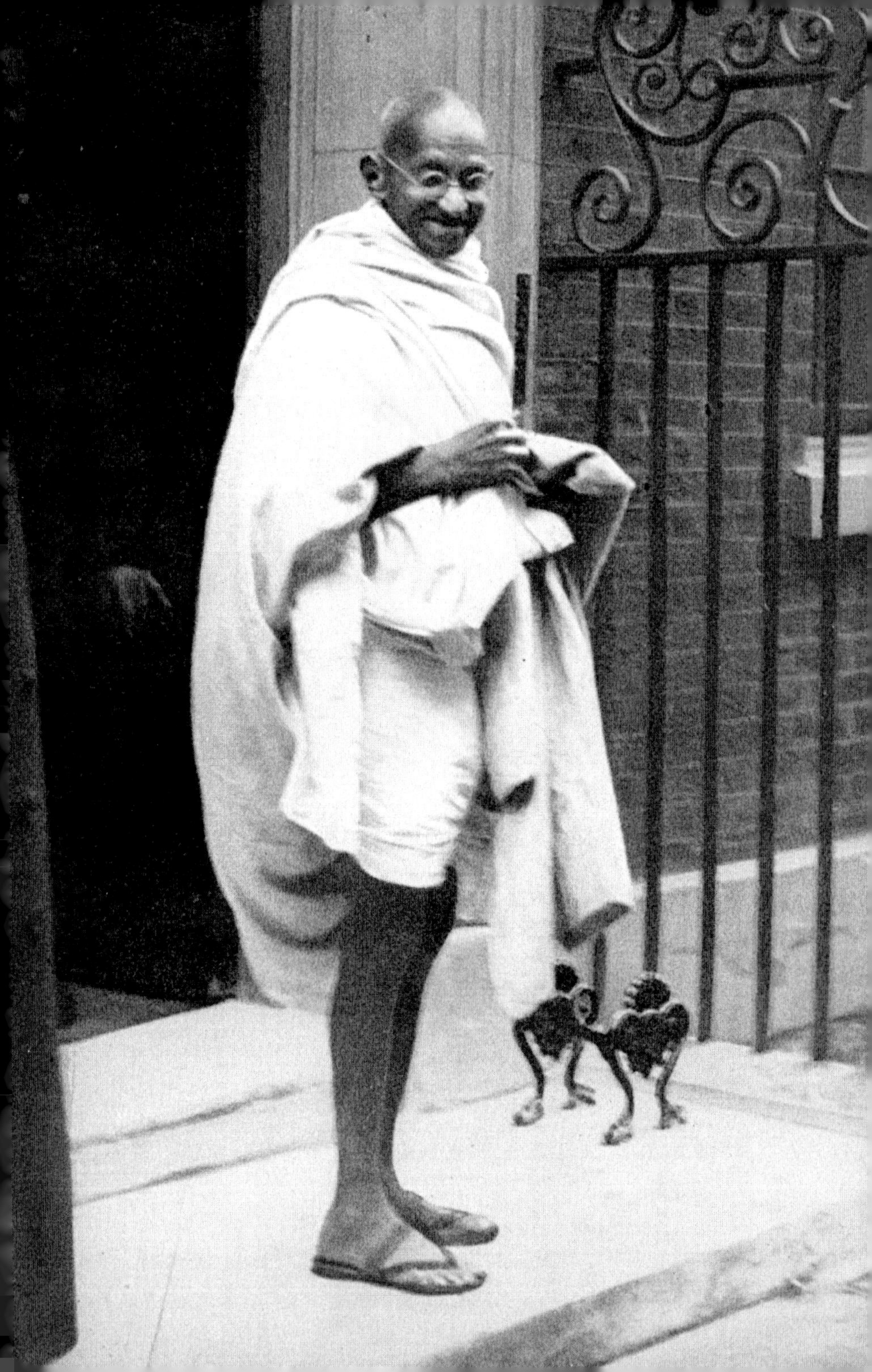

Leaving 10, Downing Street.

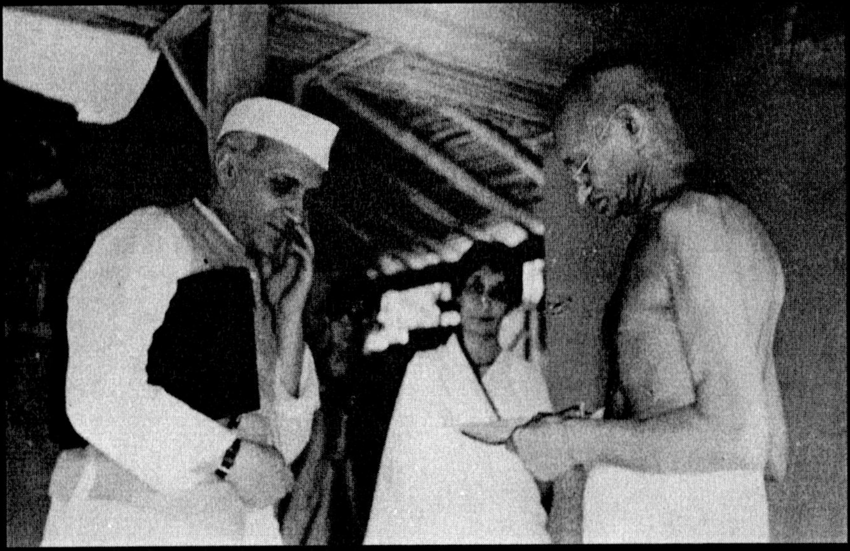

On the ashram precincts, Segaon, January 1938.

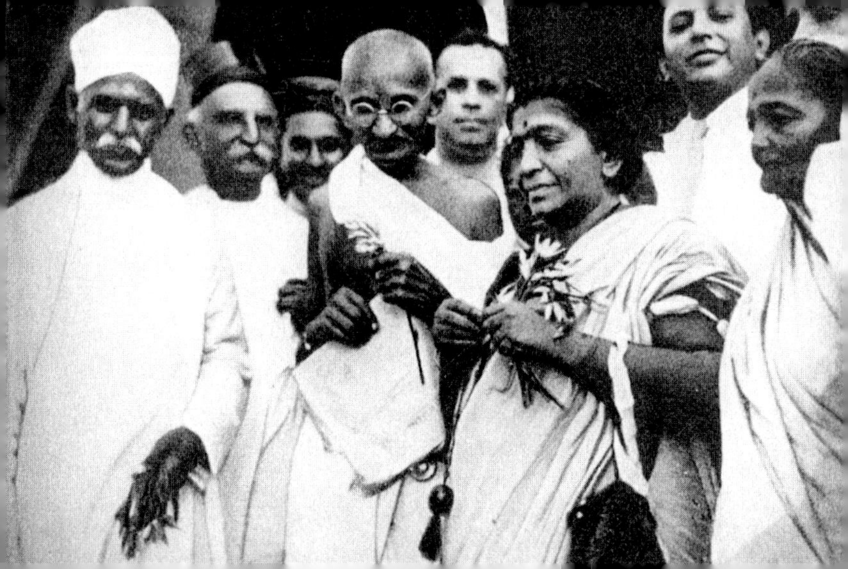

Gandhi, Kasturbai, Sarojini Naidu and Madan Mohan Malaviya in Bombay

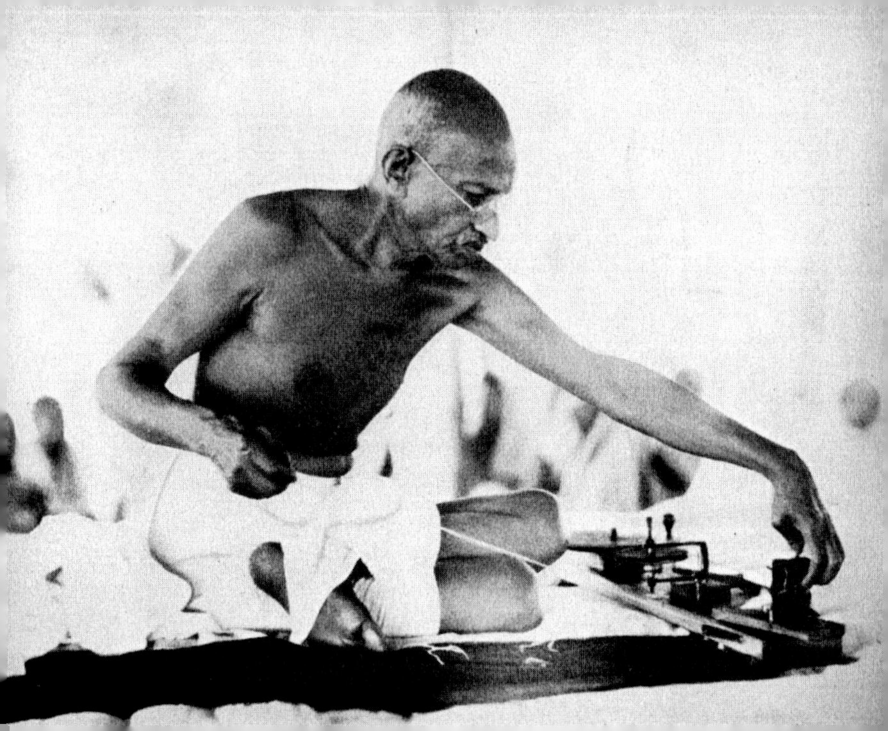

Spinning with Yerwada chakra, 1940.

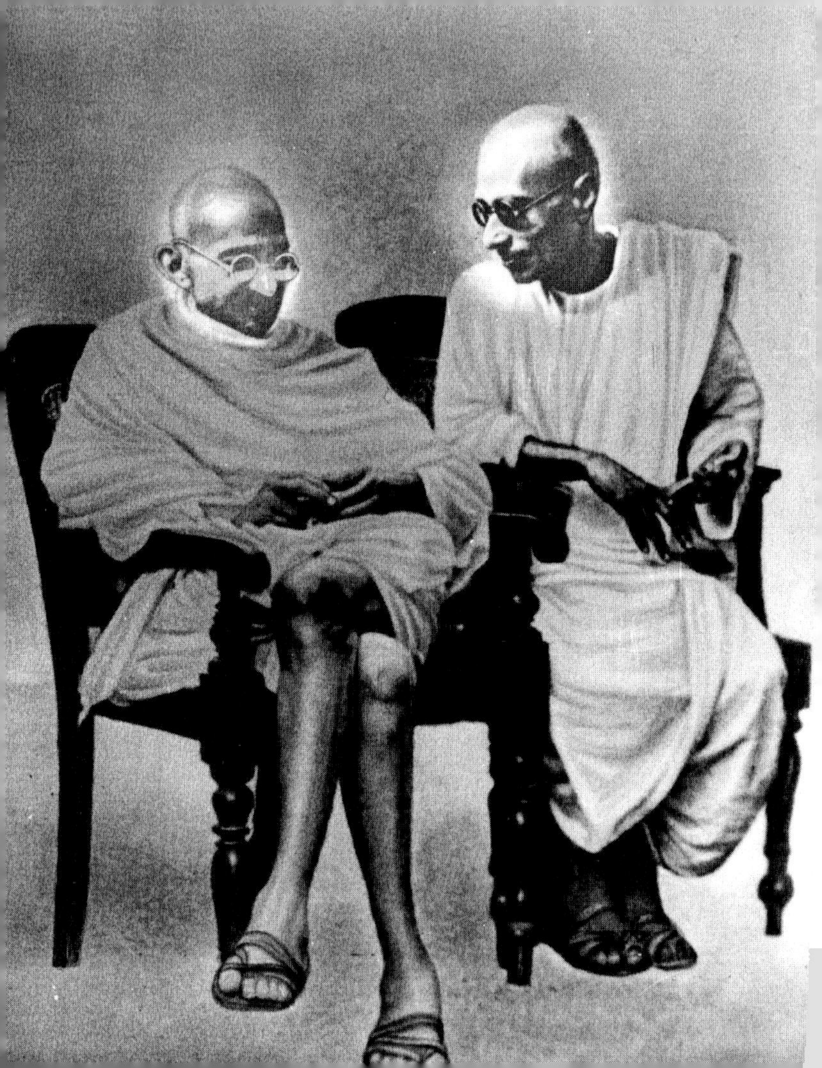

With C. Rajagopalachari.

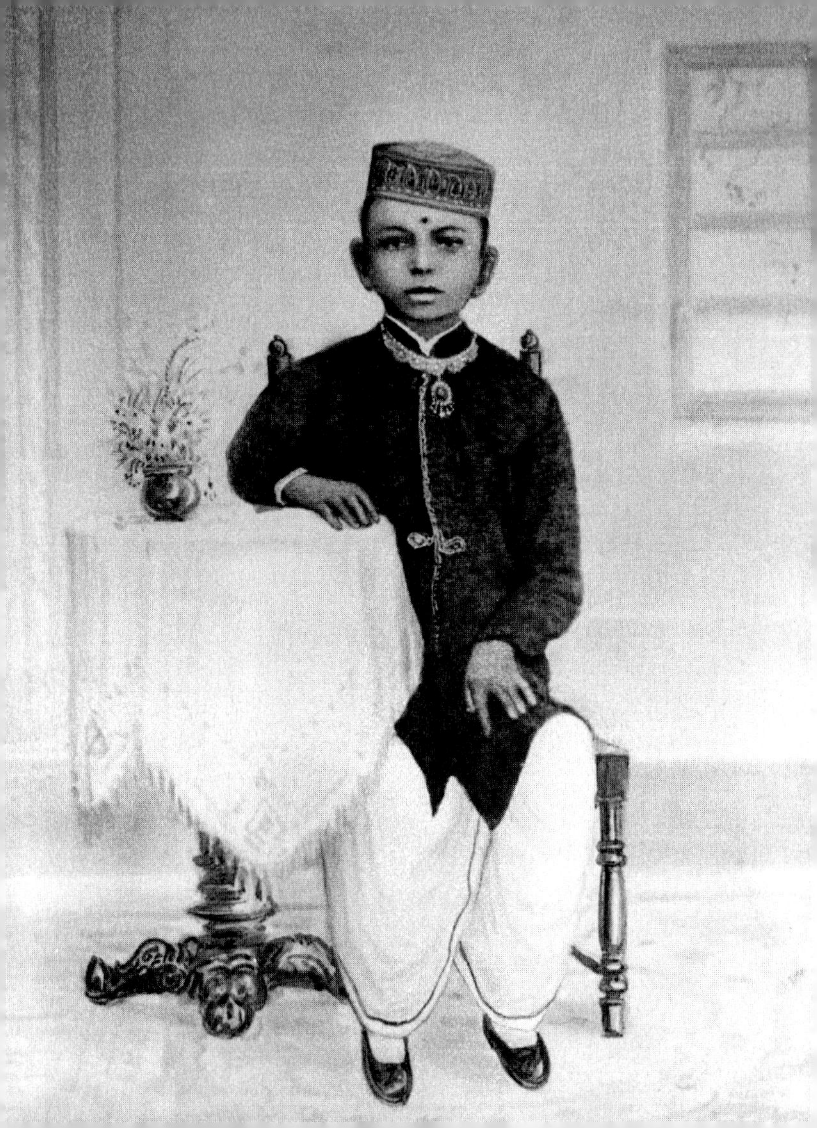

Mohandas at Porbandar, age 7.

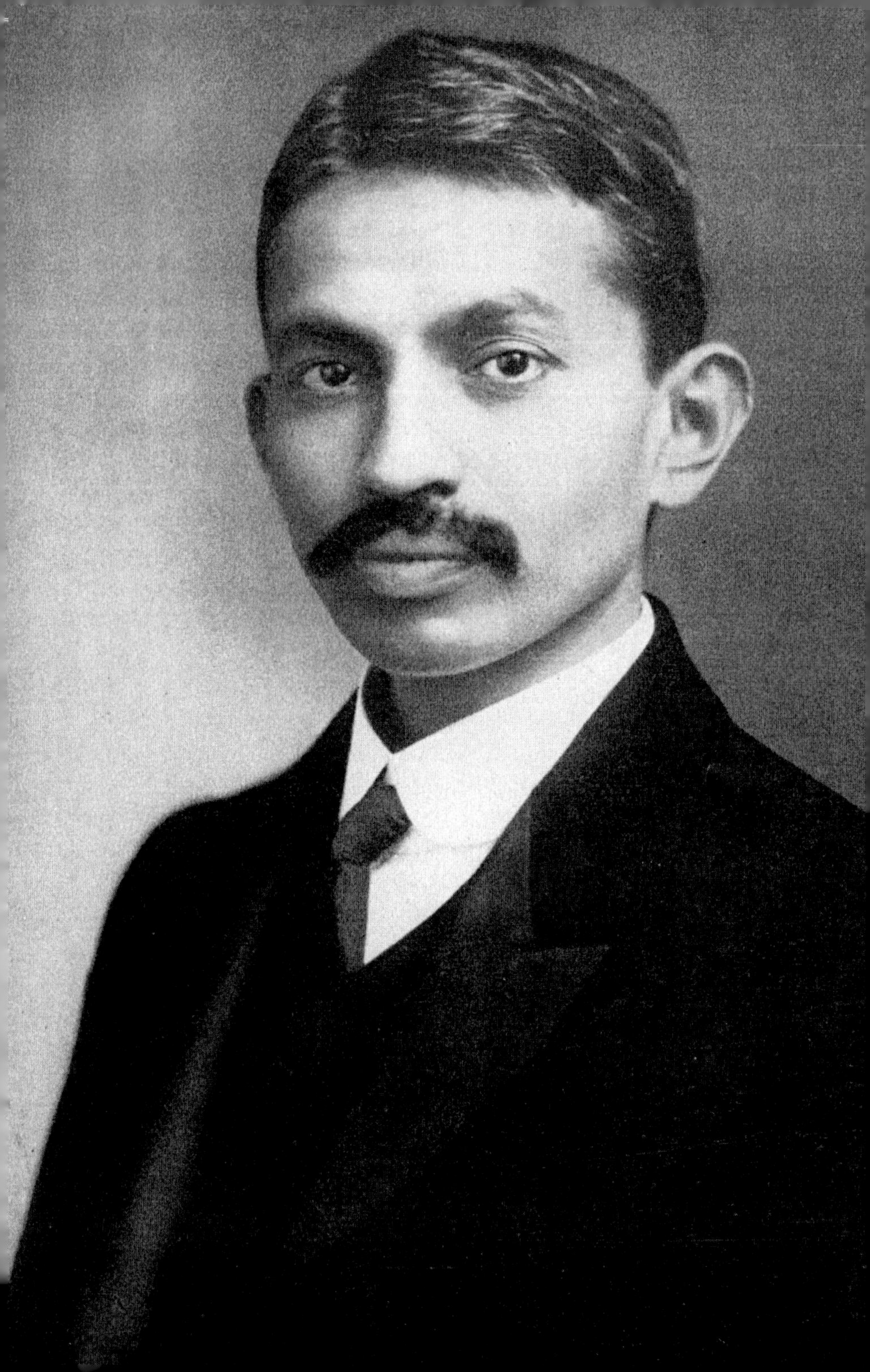

London, 1906.

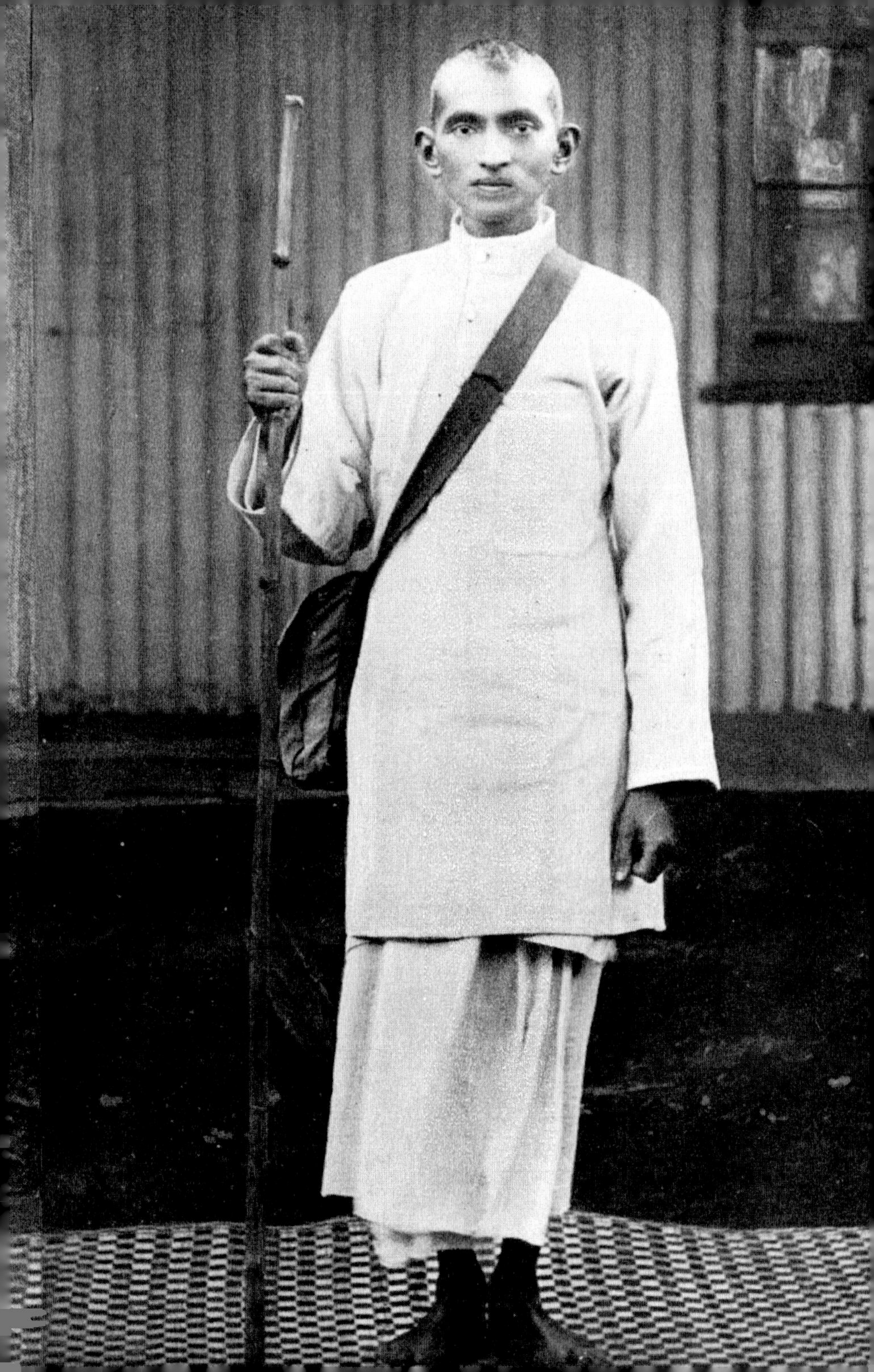

During the Satyagraha struggle, 1914.

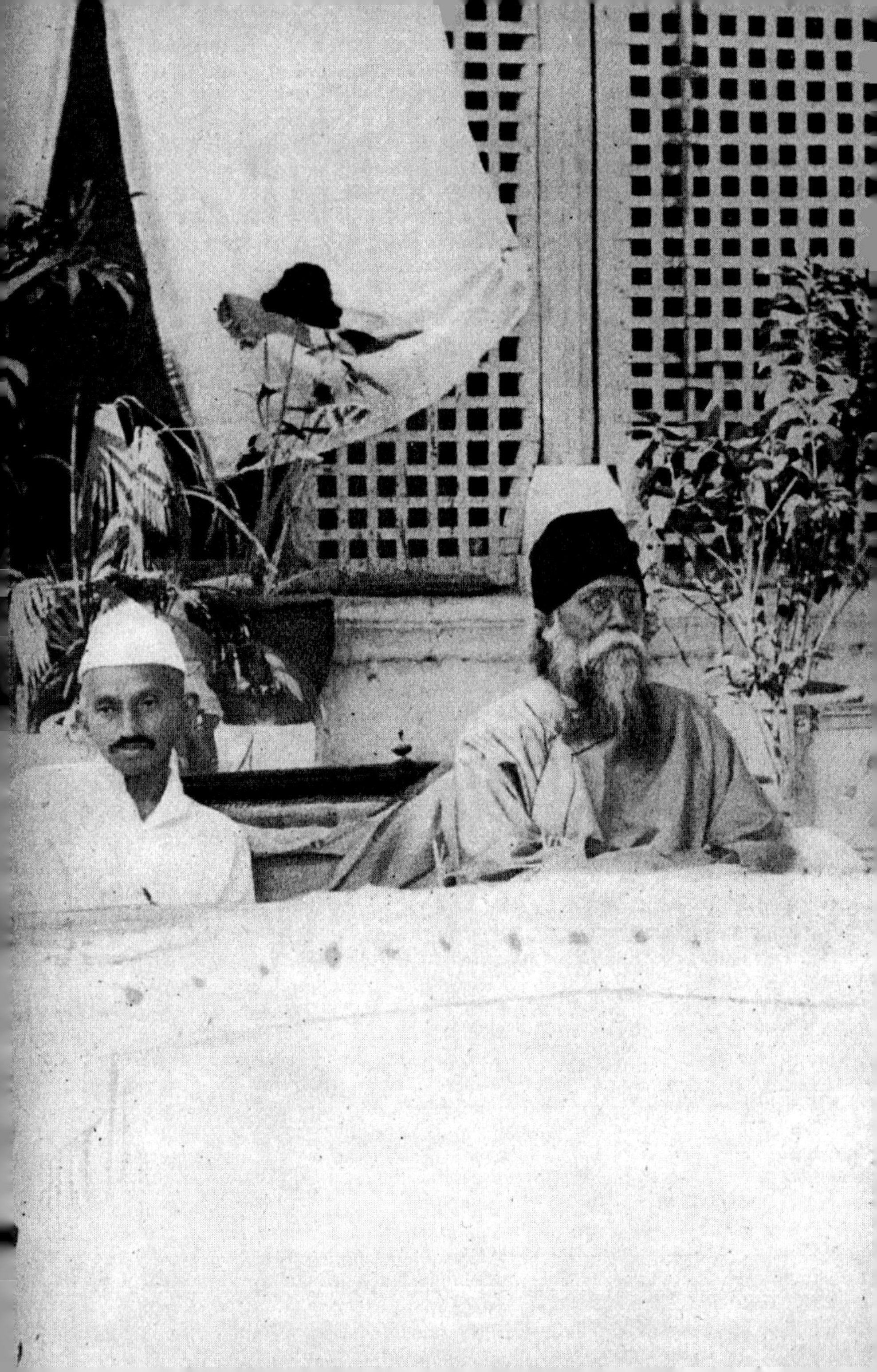

Gandhi and Tagore at the reception given to Tagore at Vanita Vishram during his visit to Ahmedabad for the sixth Gujarati Literary Conference, April 1920.

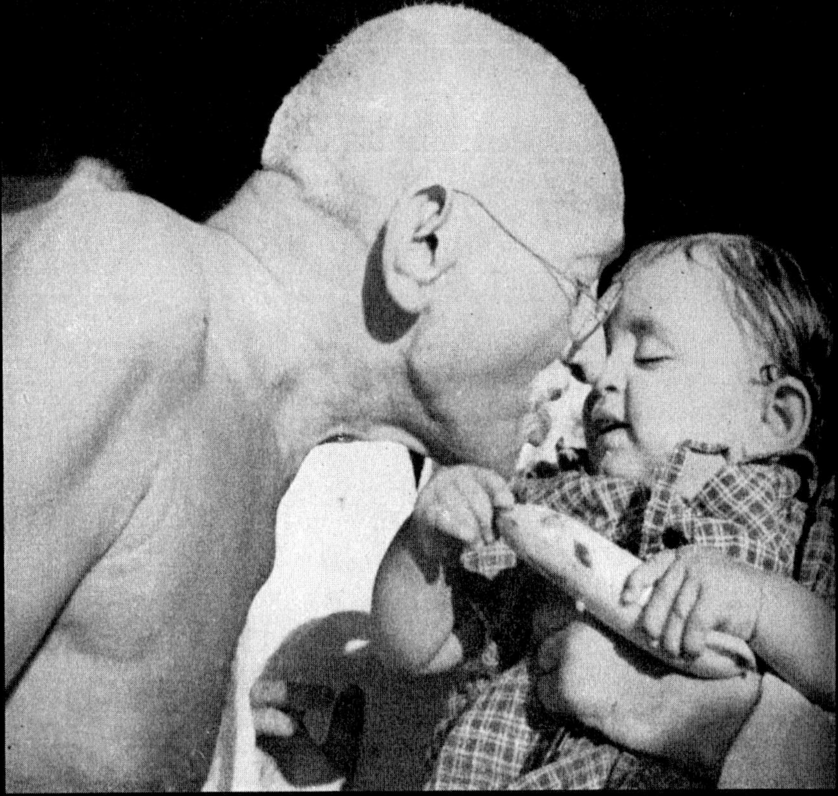

Playing with a child, Sevagram.

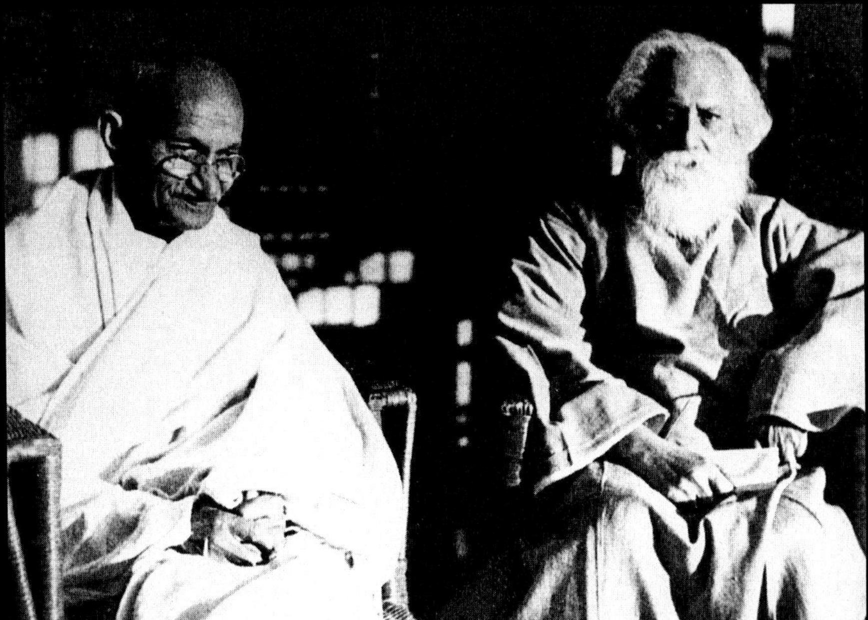

The Poet and the Mahatma,
Santiniketan.

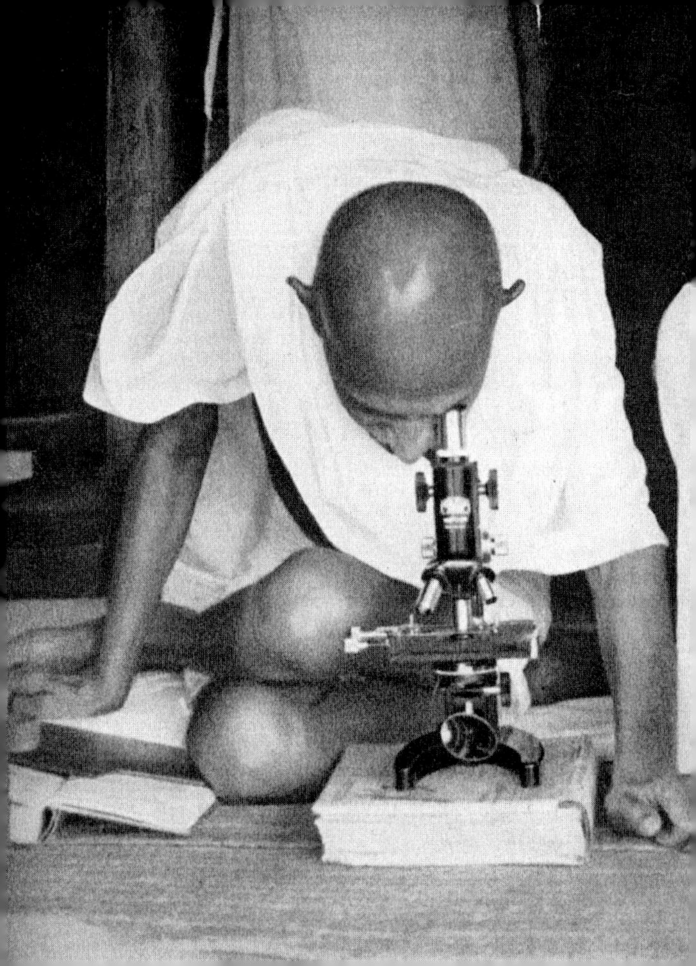

Studying the leprosy germs,
Segaon.

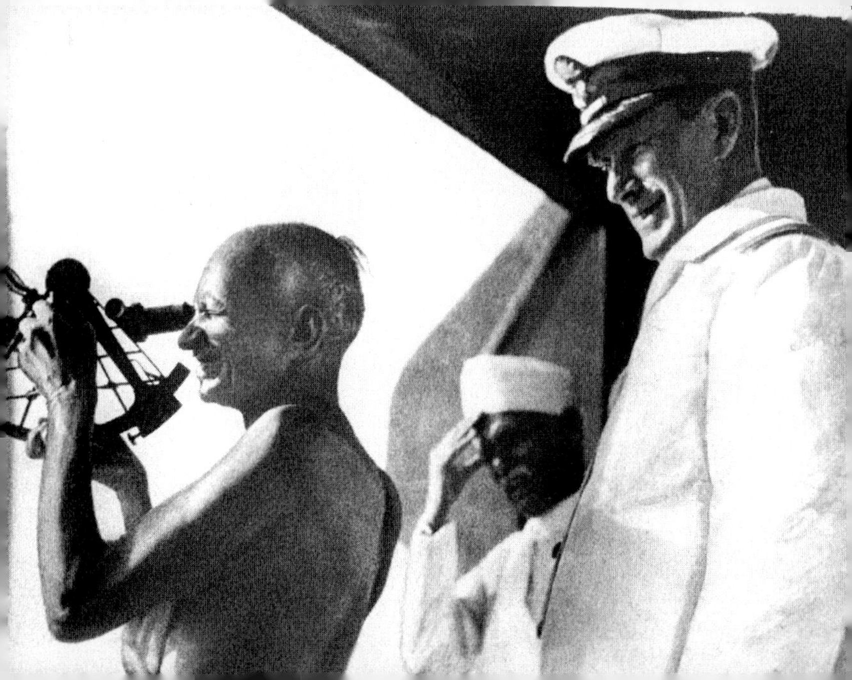

)n the deck of *S.S. Rajputana.*

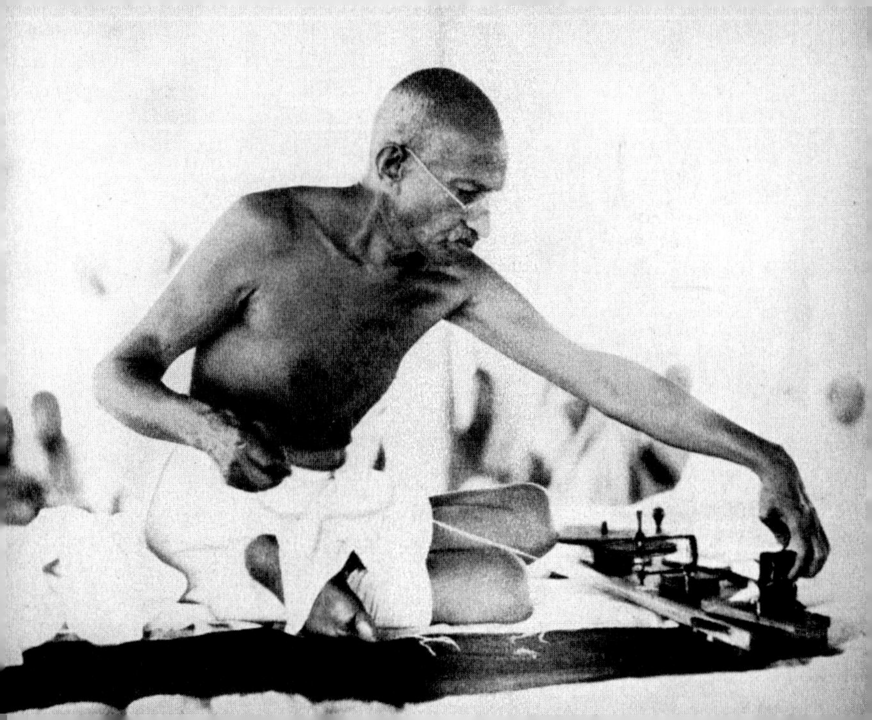

Spinning with Yerwada chakra, 1940.

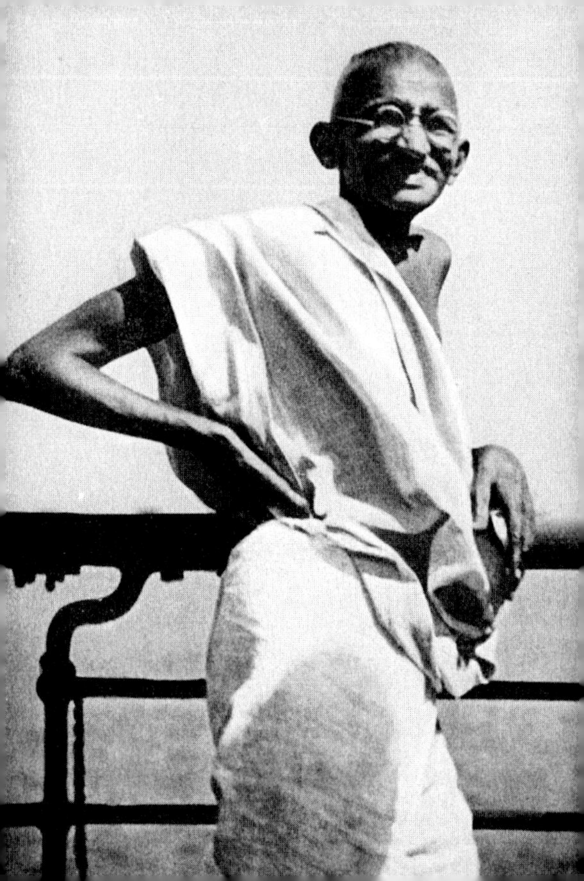

On board *S.S. Rajputana*, 1931.

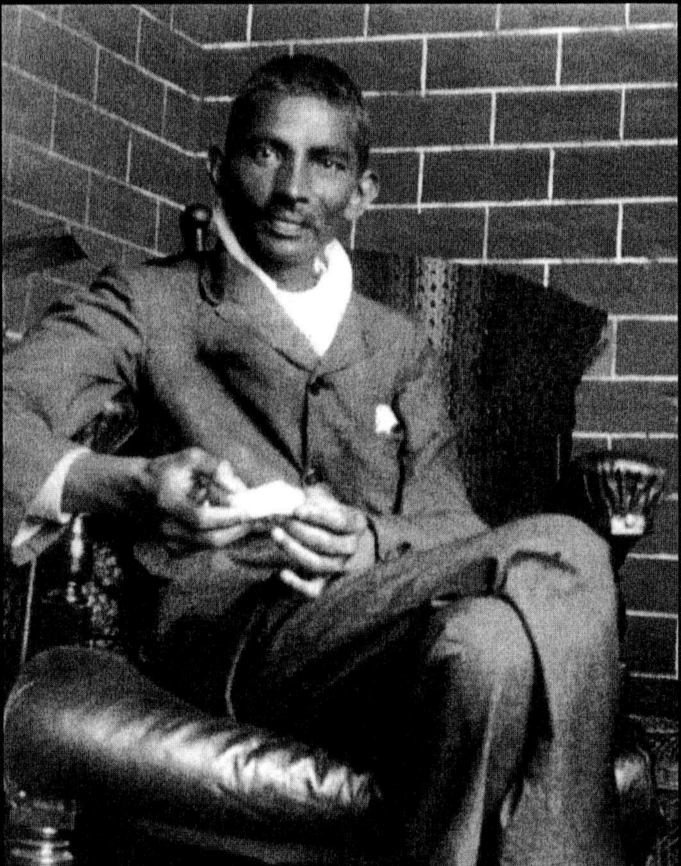

Recuperating at Rev. Joseph Doke's house after Mir Alam's assault, 1908.

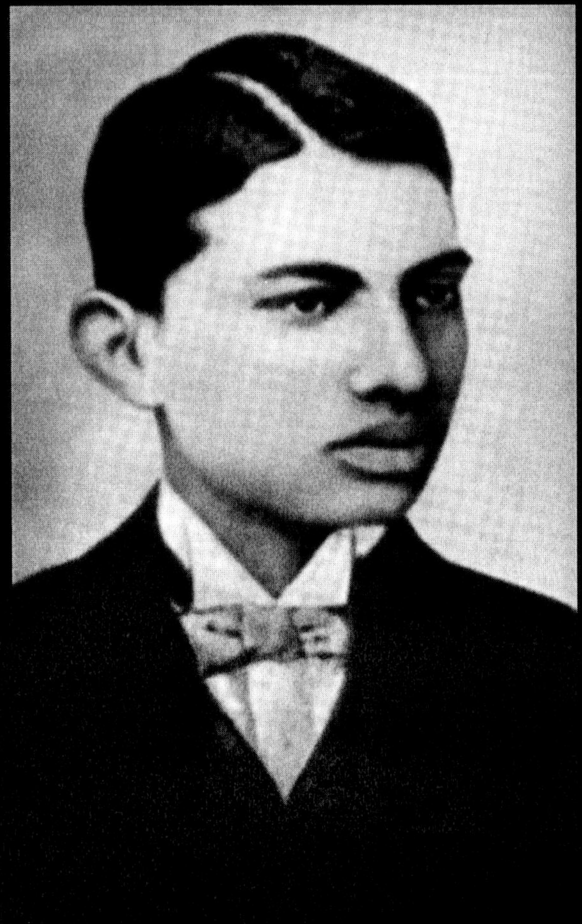

As a law student, London.

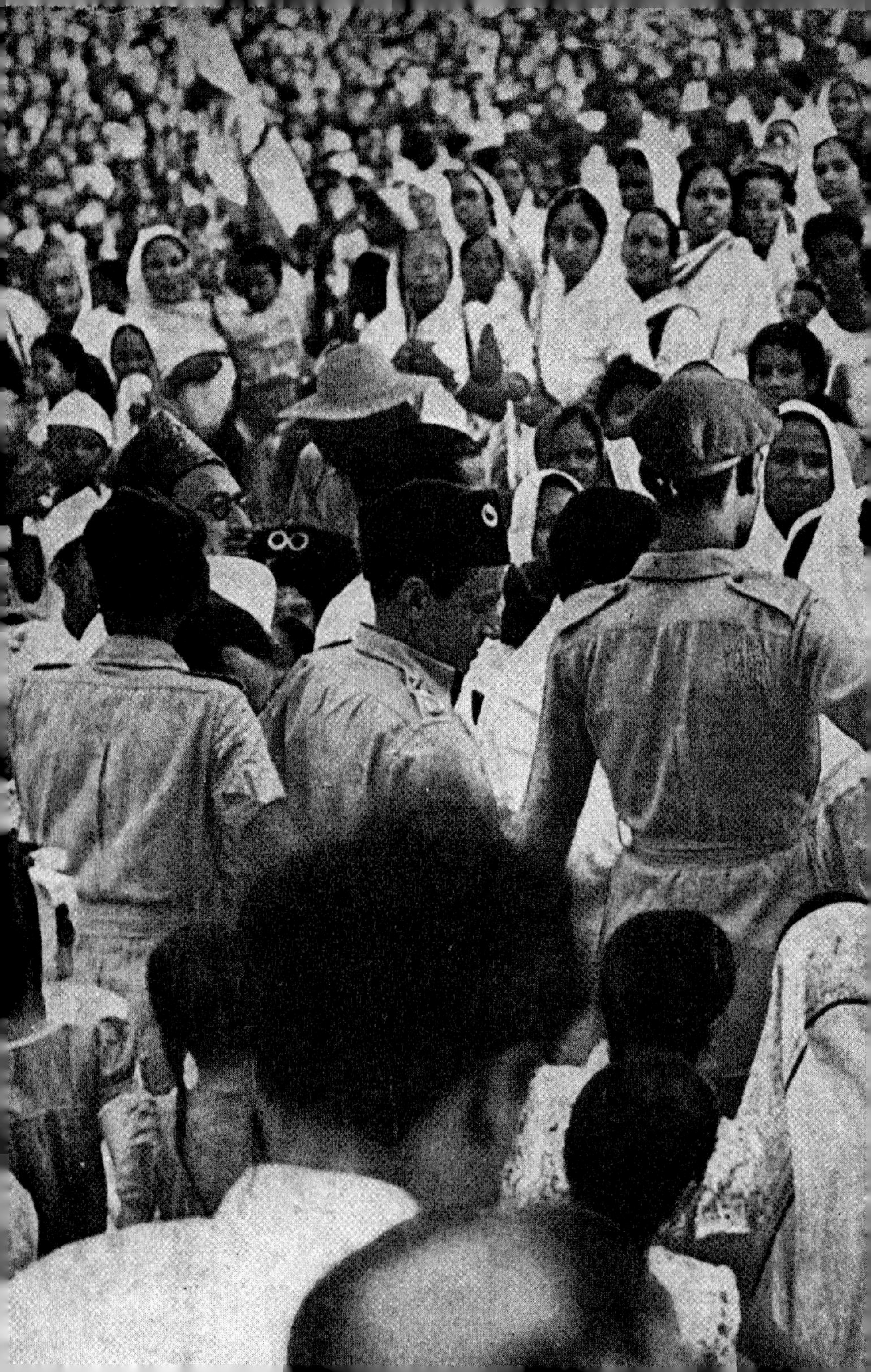

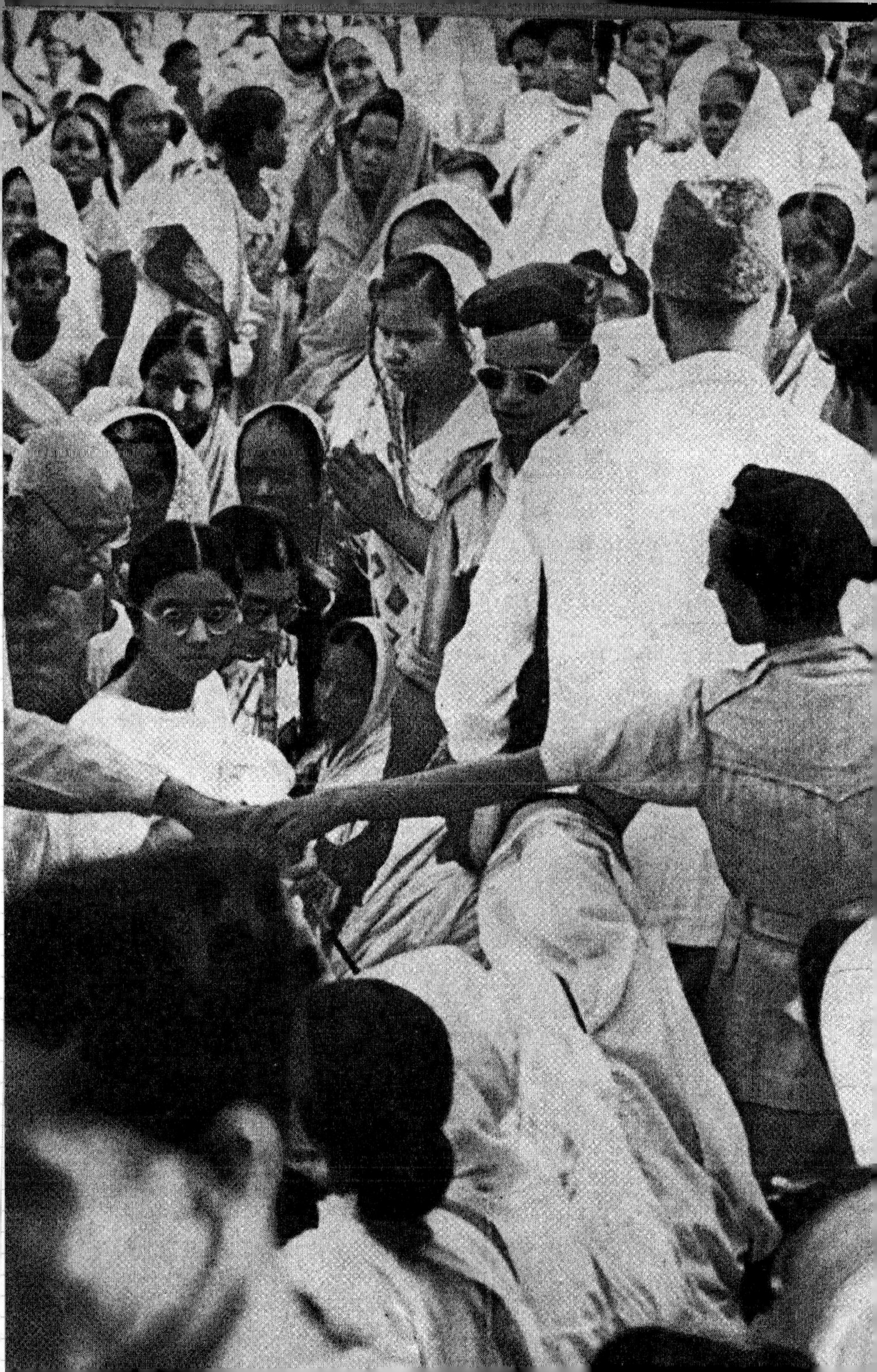

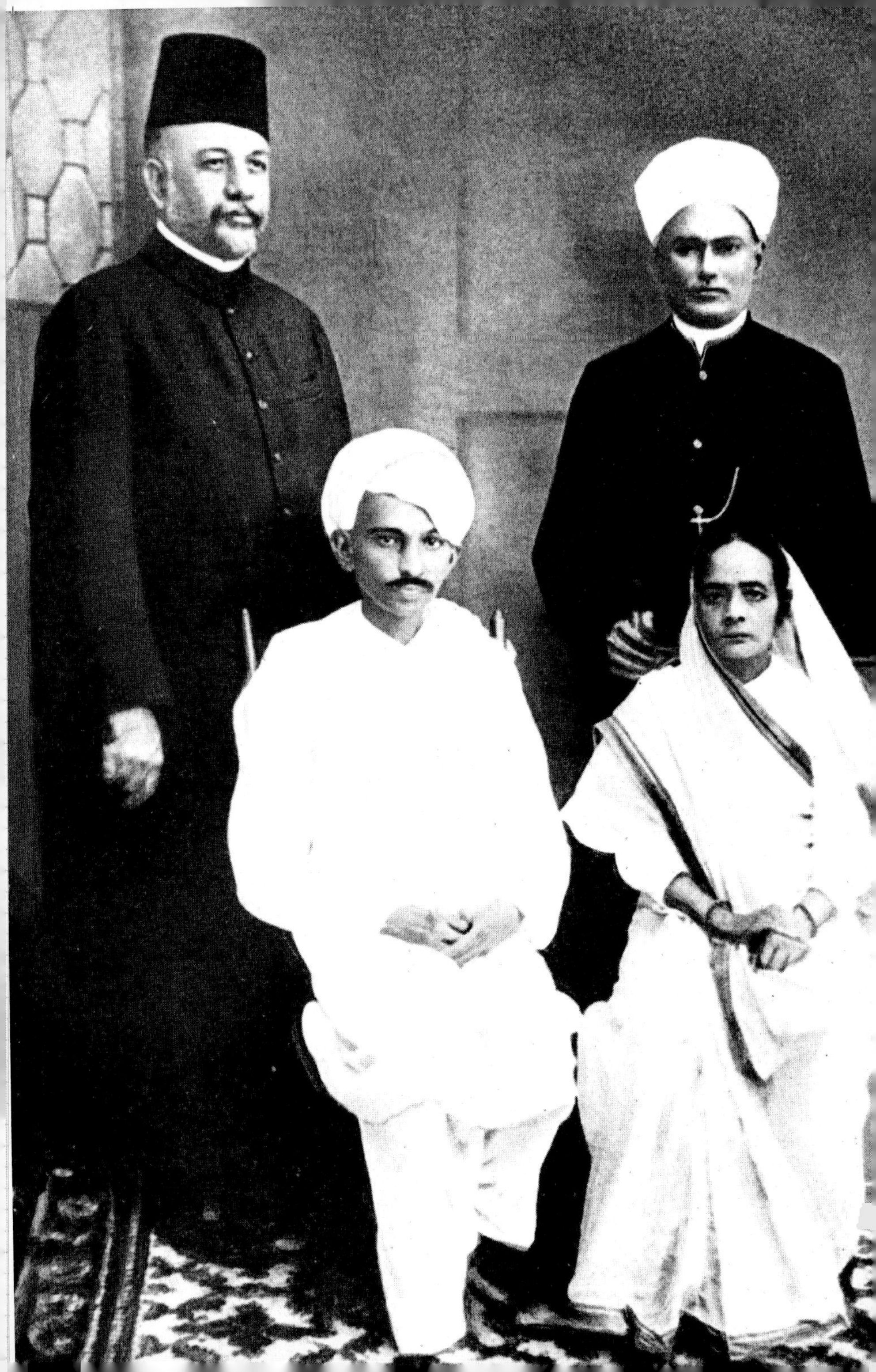

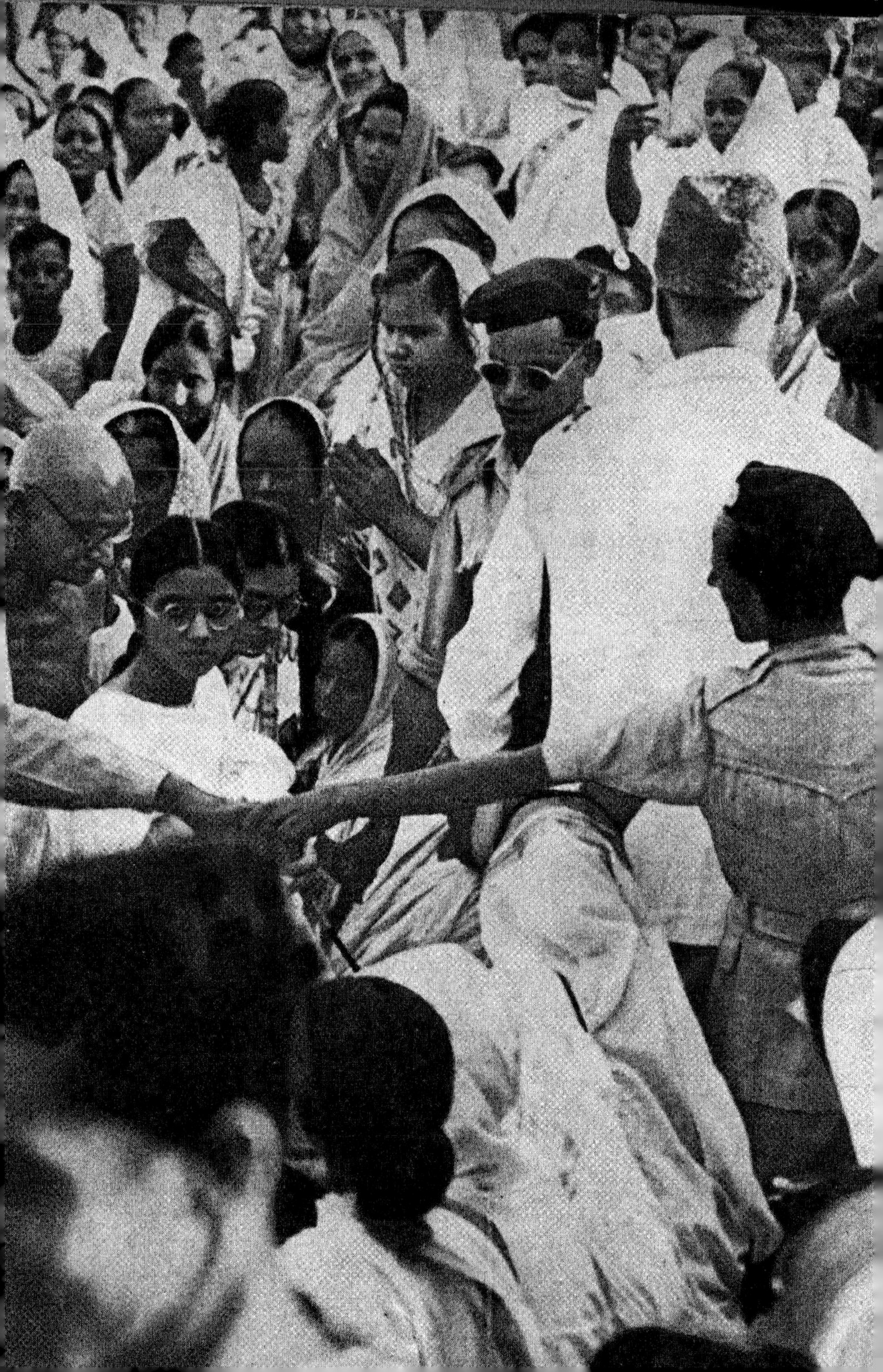

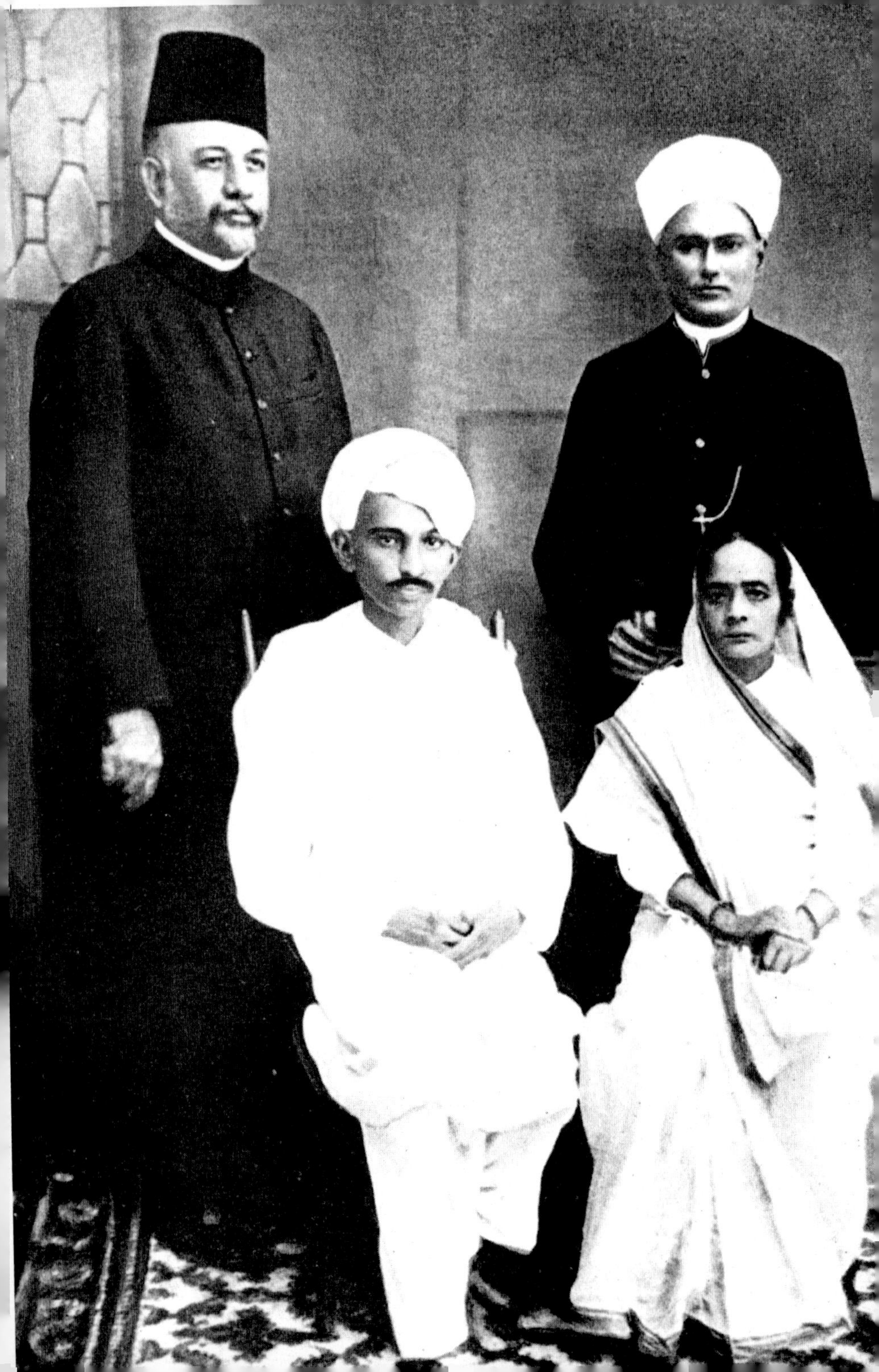

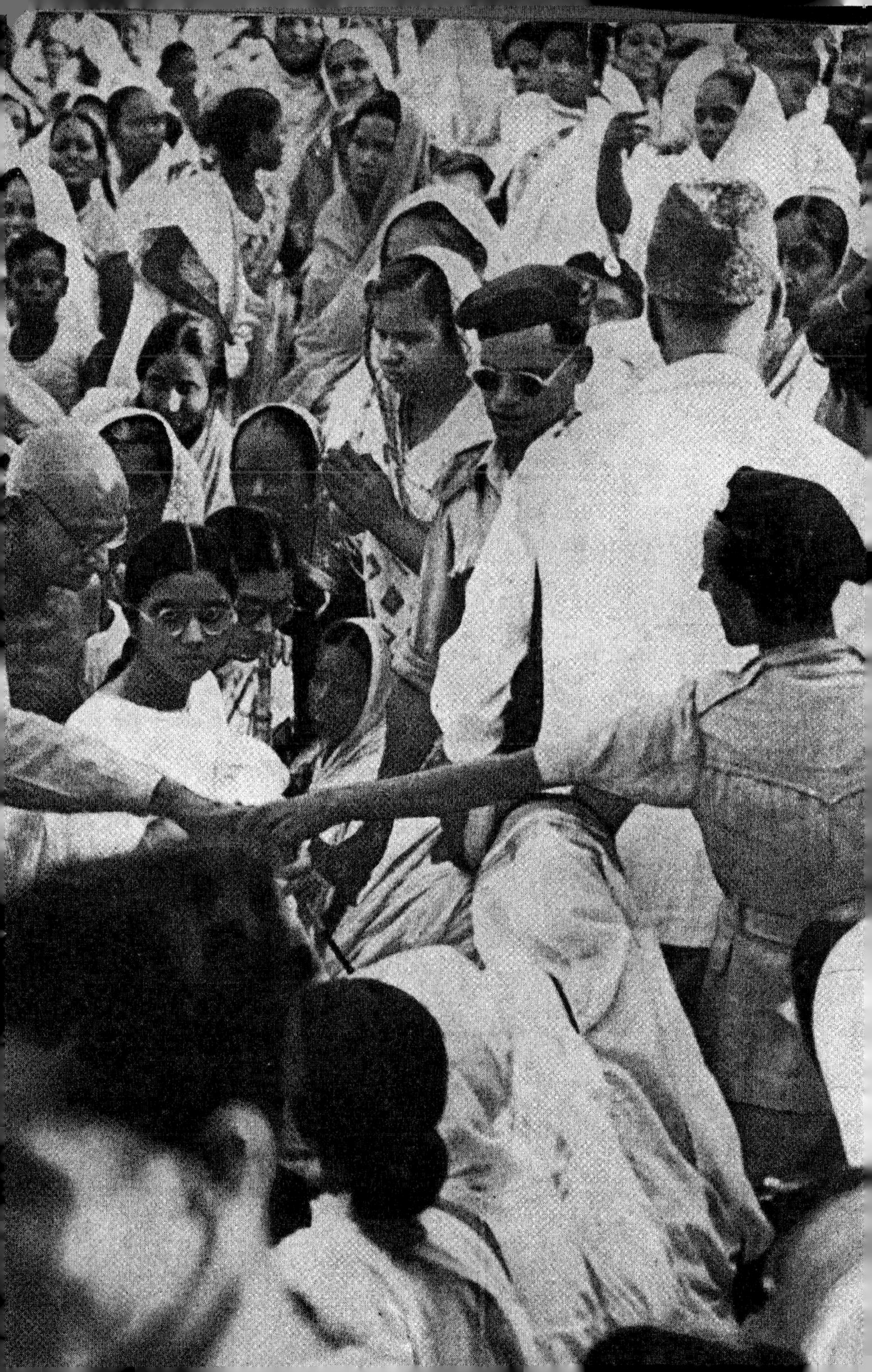

Previous page: Arriving for the Id reunion meeting at the Calcutta Maidan, August 1947.

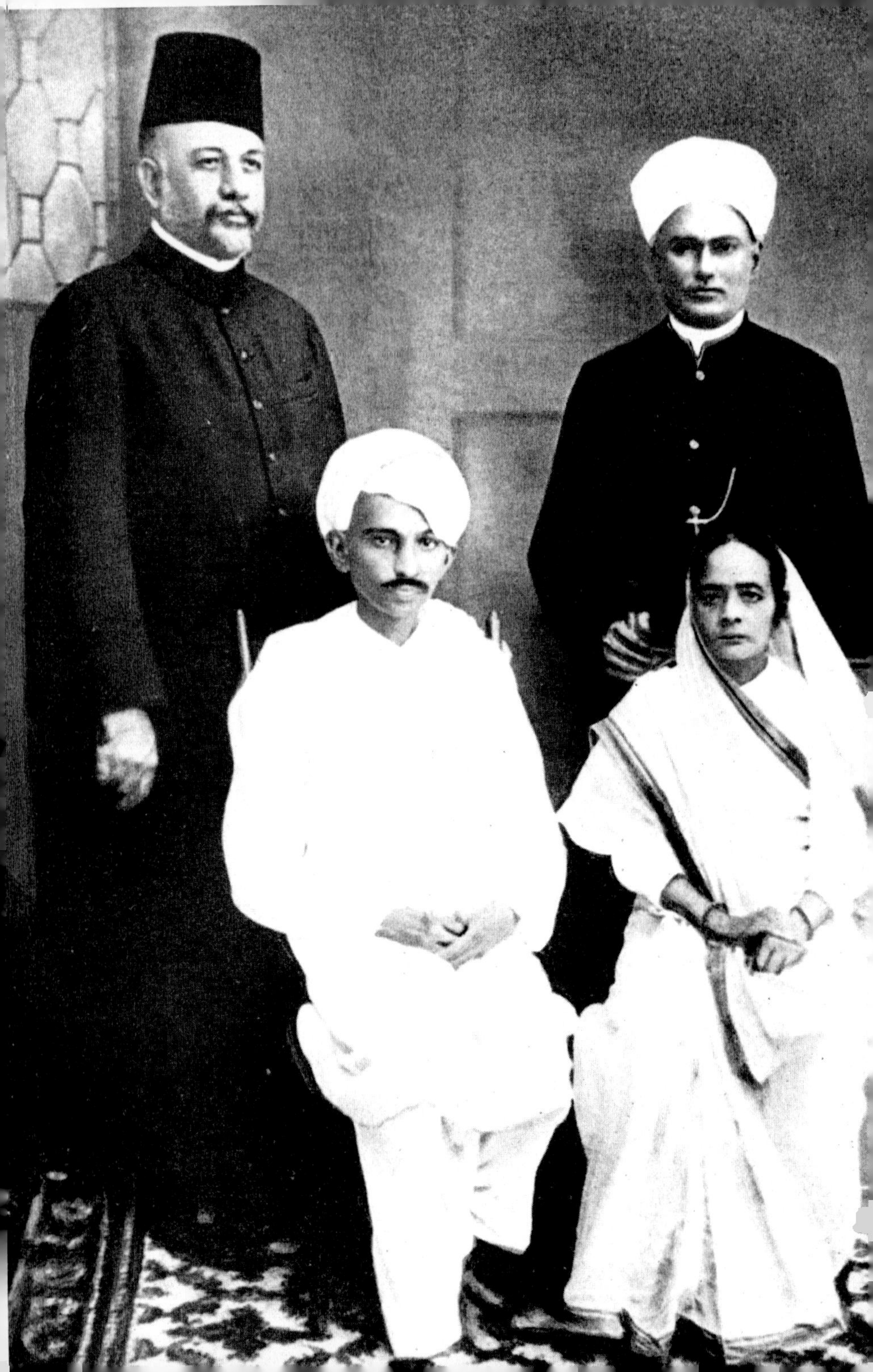

Gandhi and Kasturbai with G.A. Natesan at Madras, 1915.

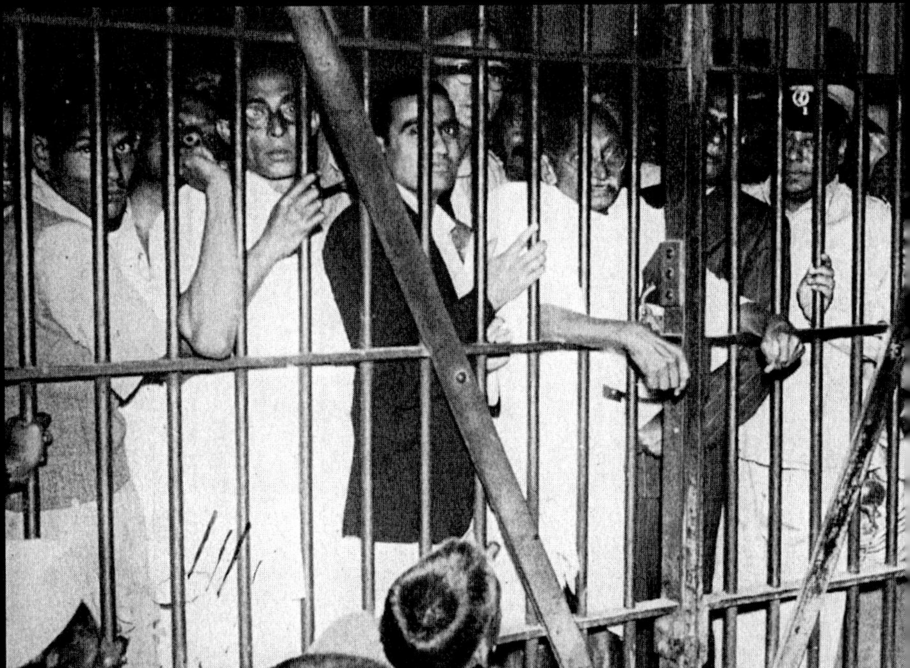

With the political prisoners at Dum Dum Central Jail, Calcutta, January 17, 1946.

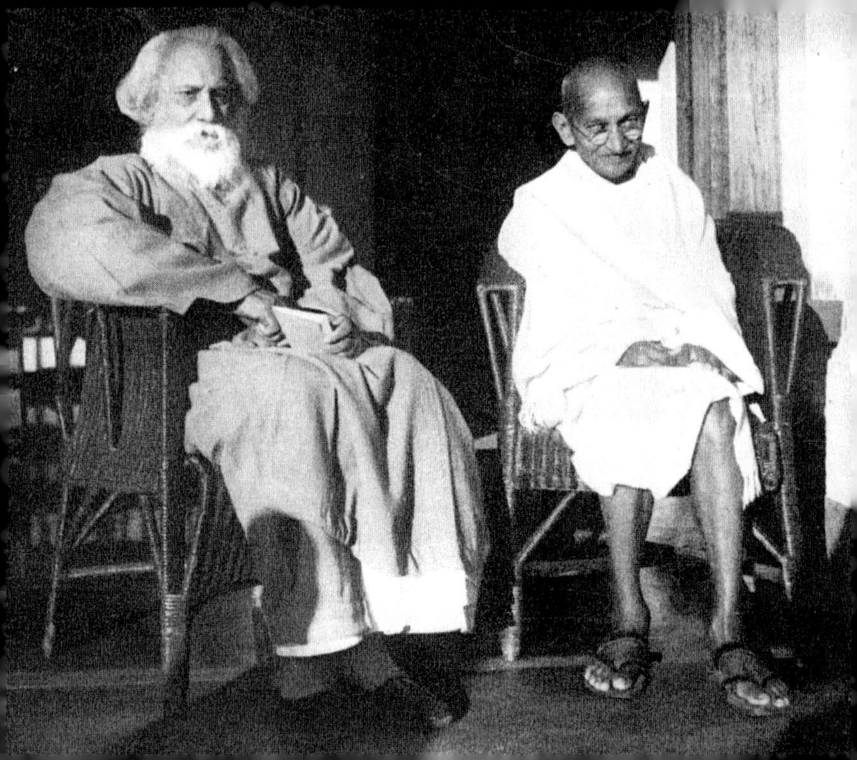

The Poet and the Mahatma,
Santiniketan.

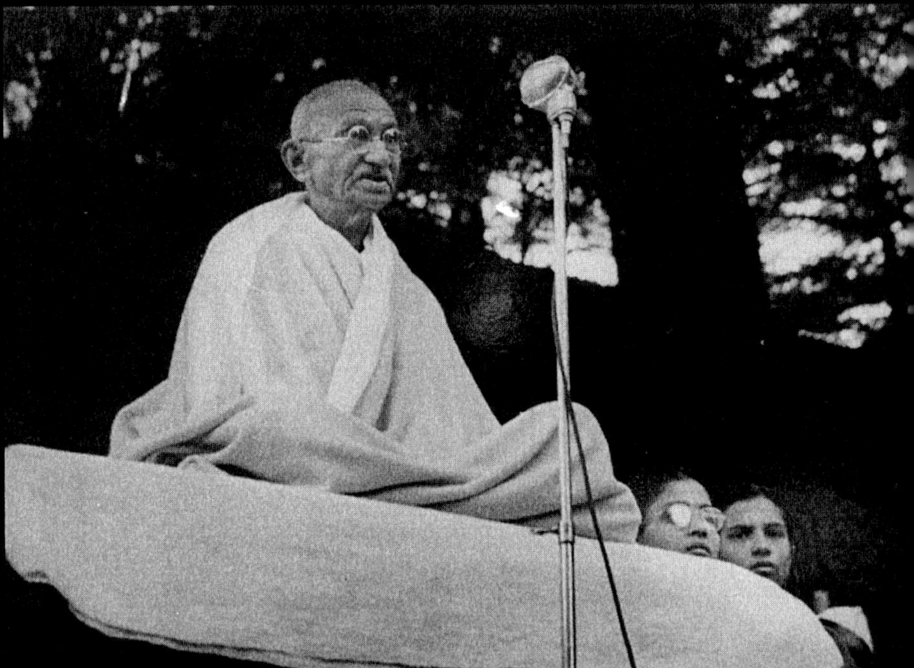

At a prayer meet.

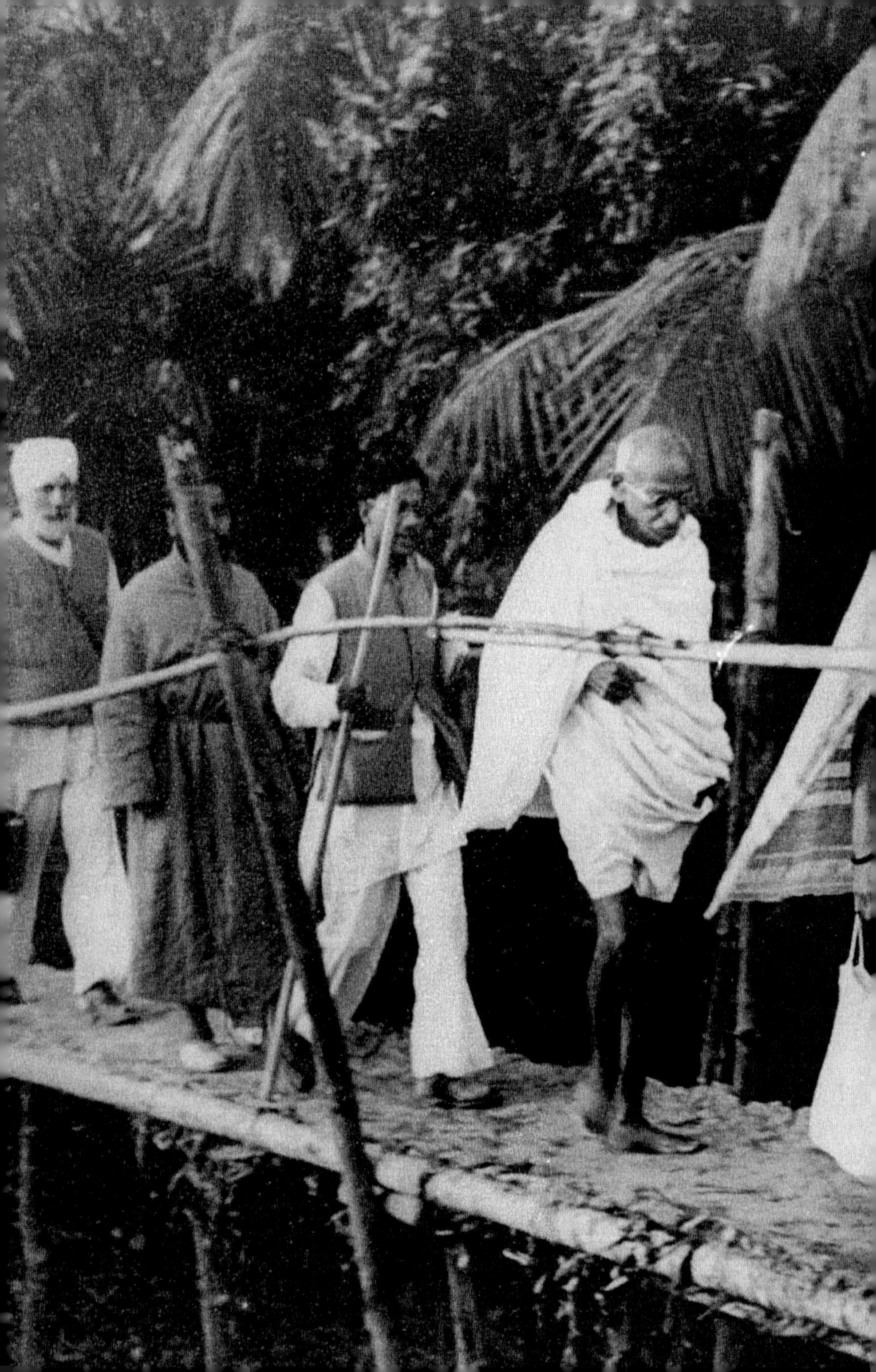

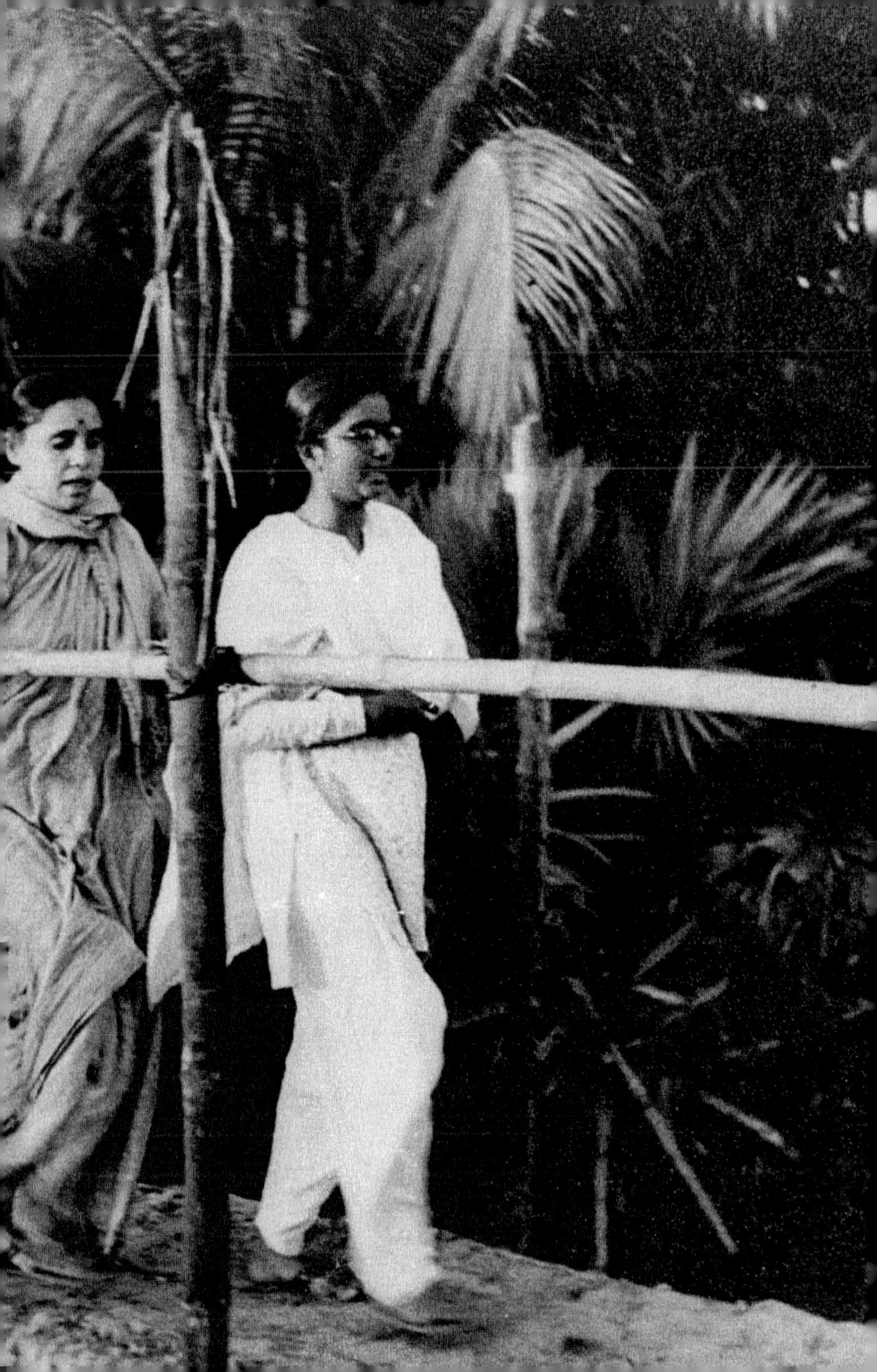

Previous page: During Noakhali march.

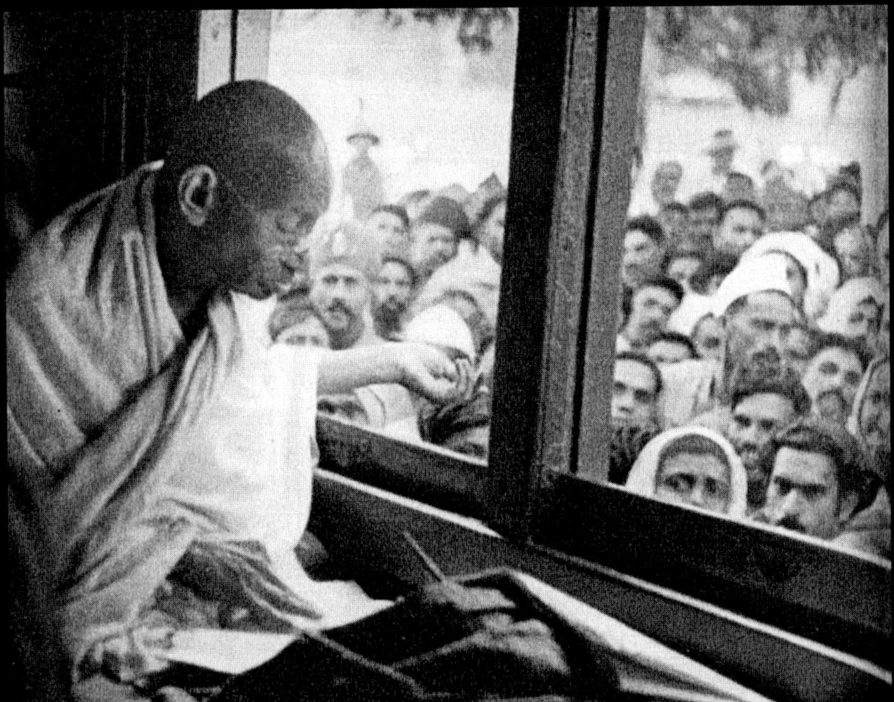

On the way to Bombay,
September 8, 1944.

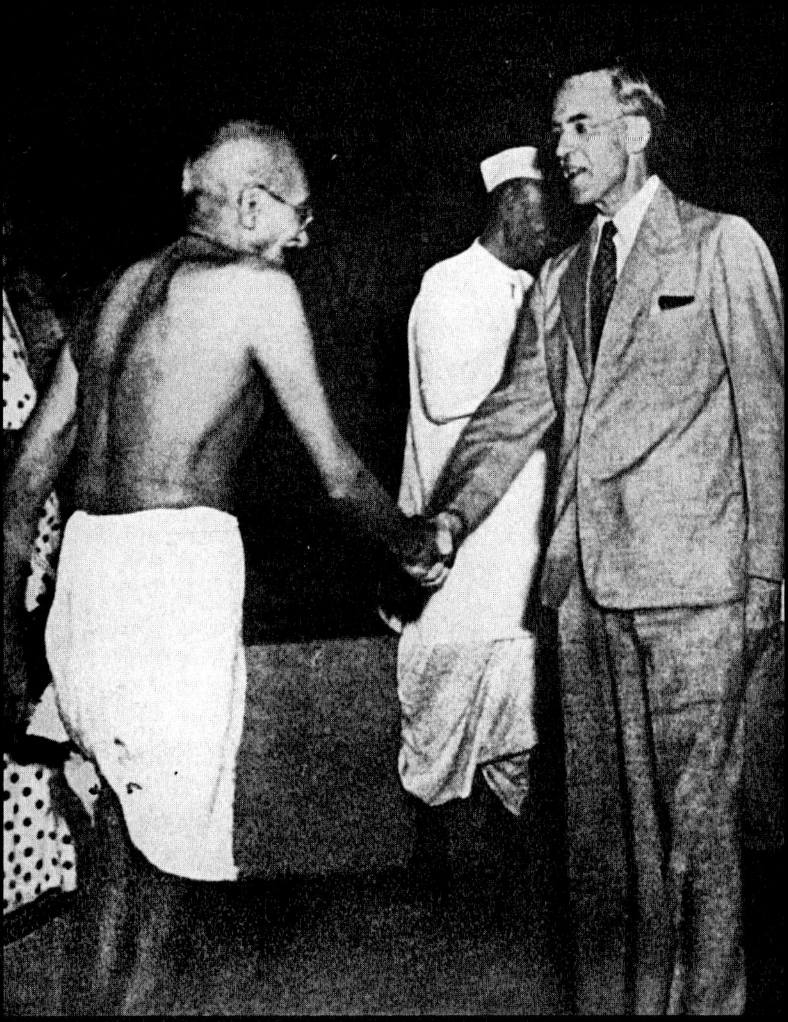

Gandhi greets Sir Stafford Cripps at the Bhangi colony, Delhi, April 1946.

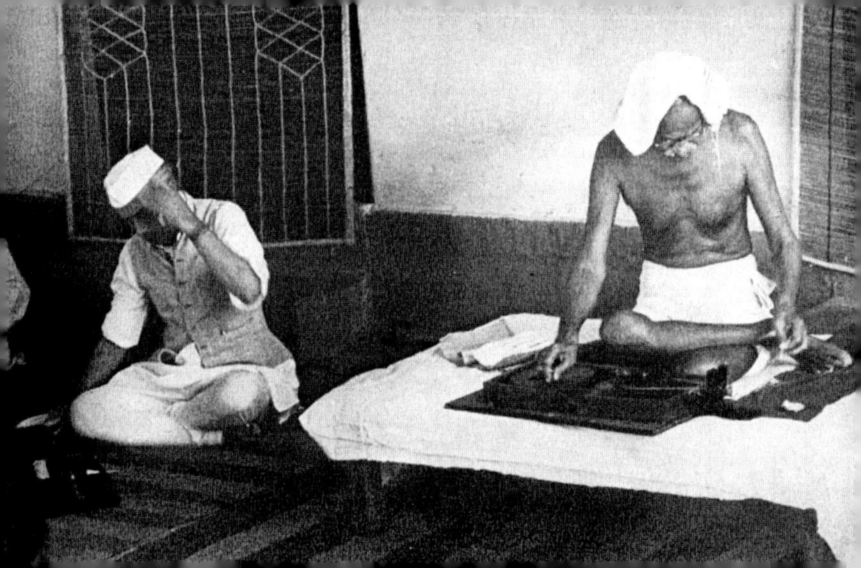

Gandhi and Nehru at the mass spinning during the National Week, Delhi, April 1946.

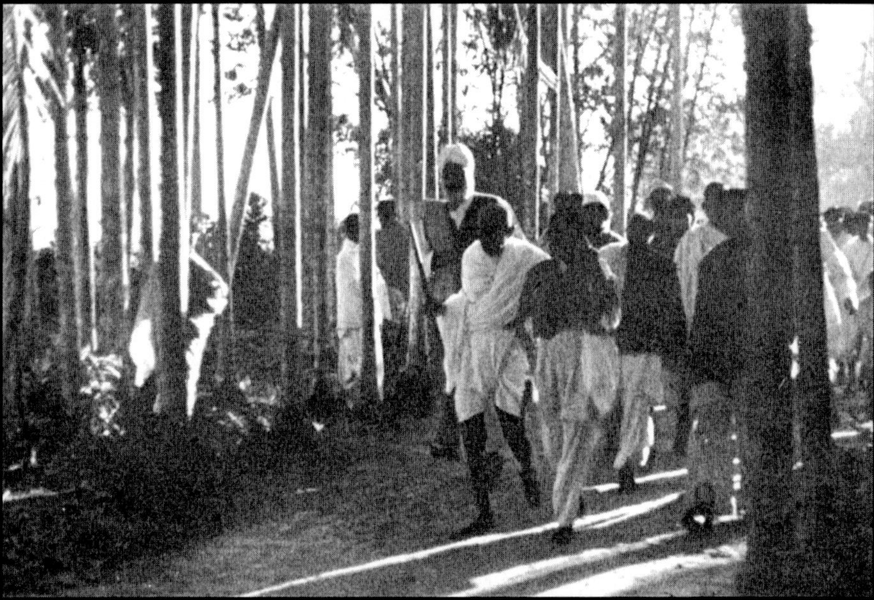

During the Noakhali march.

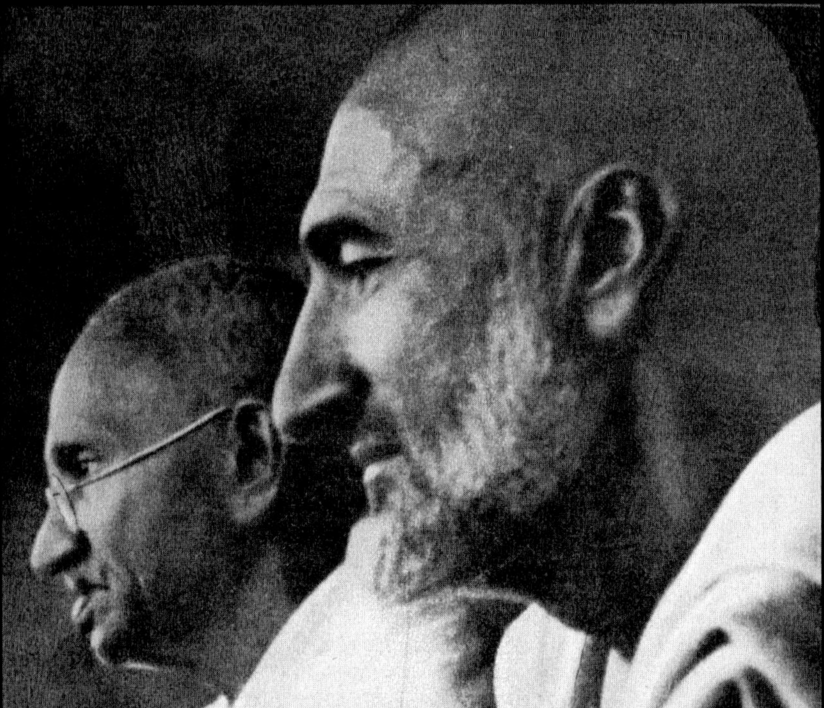

Gandhi with Ghaffar Khan, October 1938.

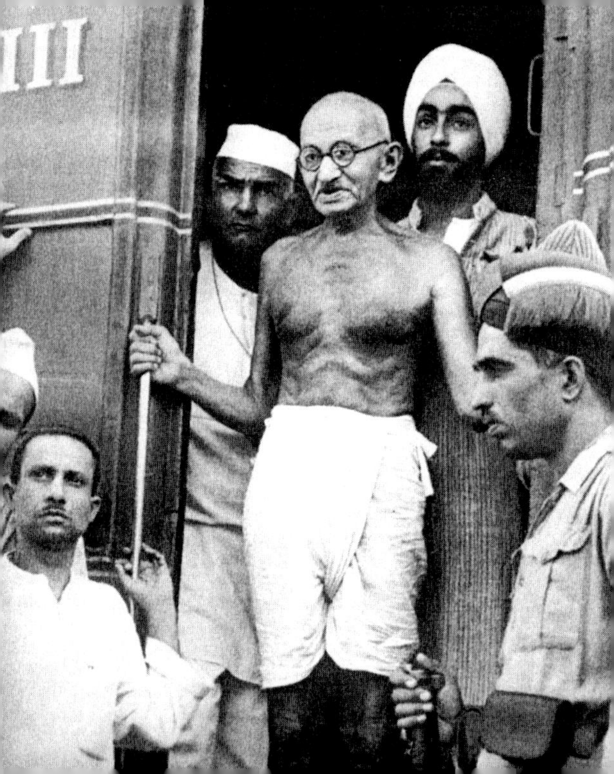
III

At Lahore railway station on his way to Kashmir, 1947.

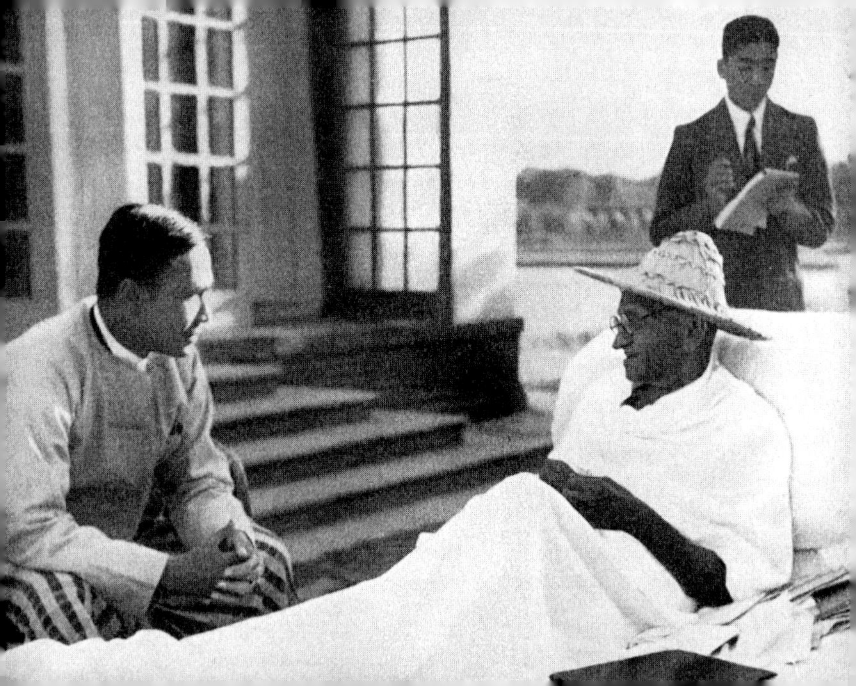

Thakin Nu, the premier of Burma, with Gandhi, Delhi, December 4, 1947.

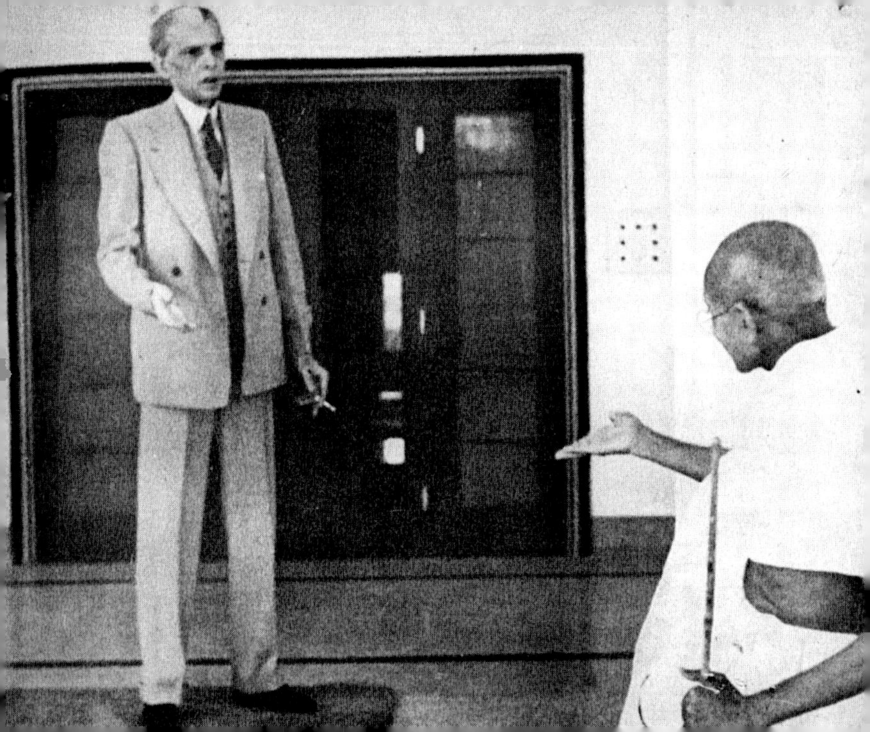

With M.A. Jinnah.

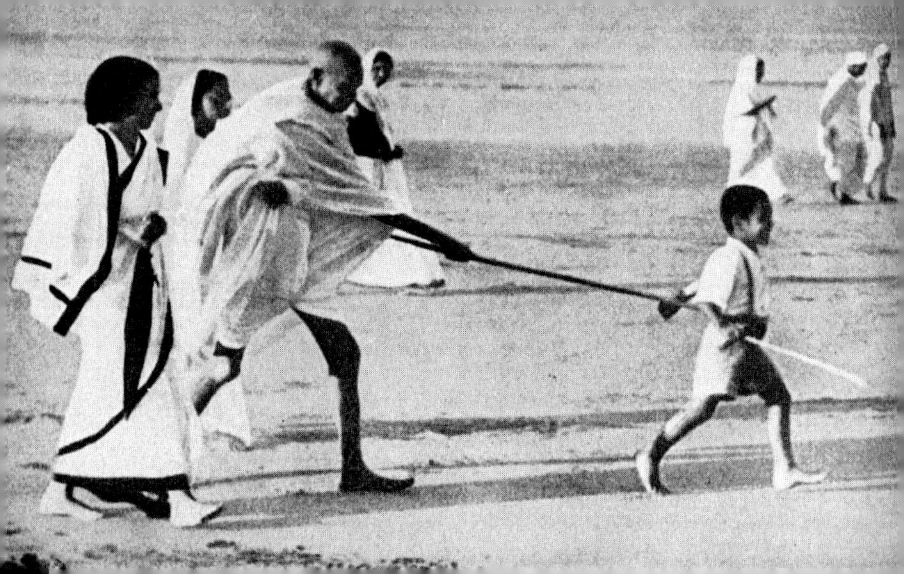

Gandhi on the Juhu beach, Bombay, during his convalescence, December 1937.

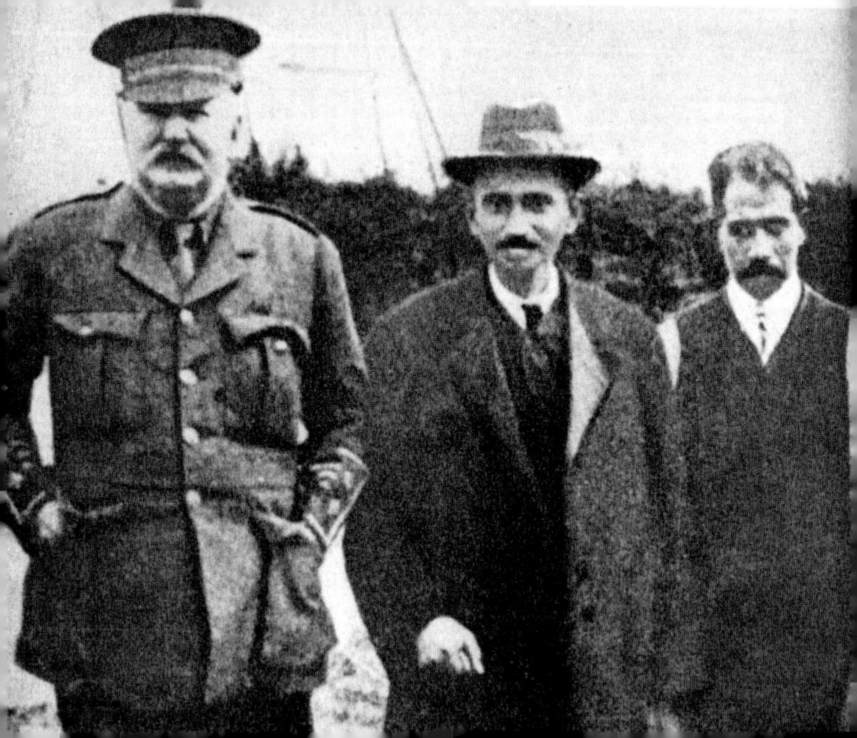

During the First World War, as an organiser of the Indian Ambulance Corps, London, 1914.

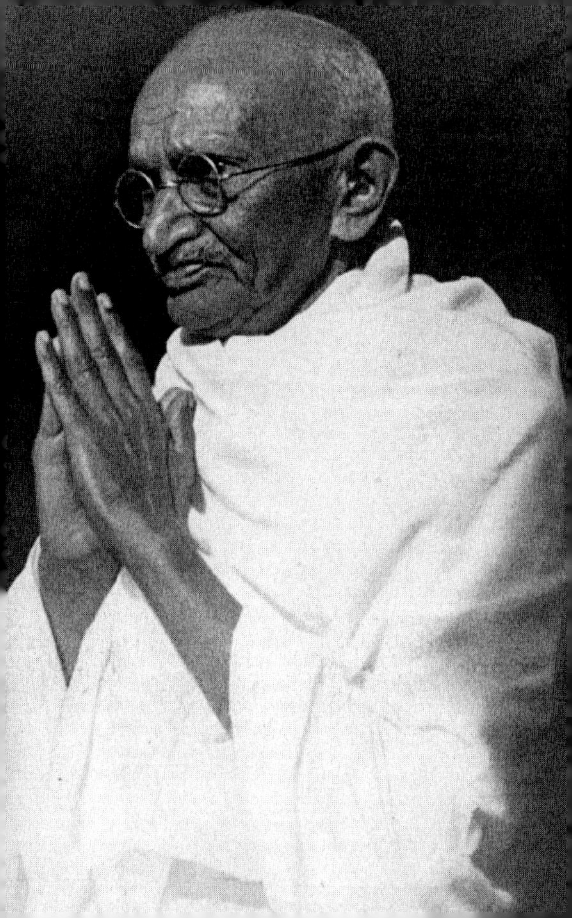

Greeting the people.

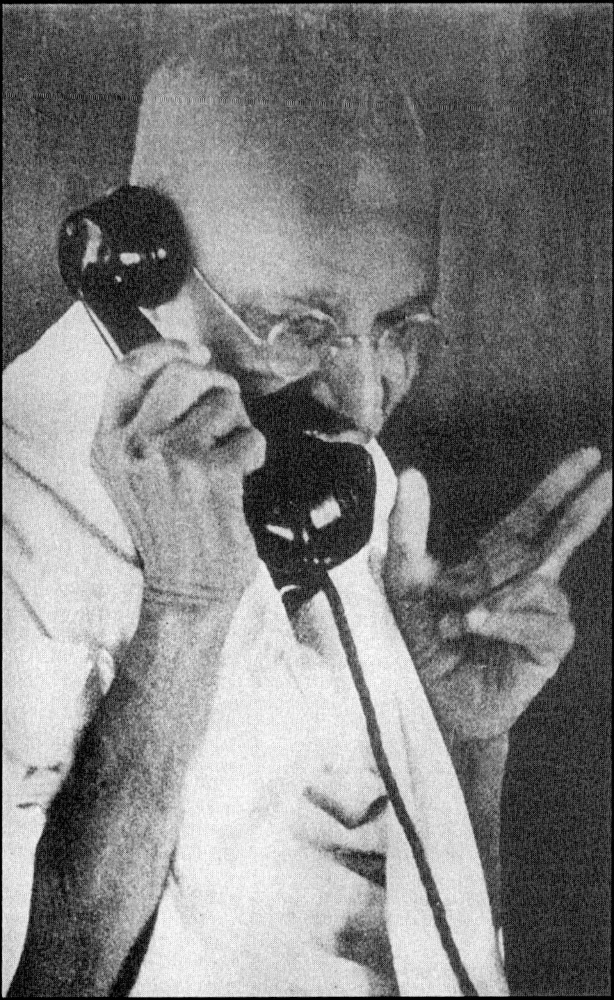

t Sevagram.

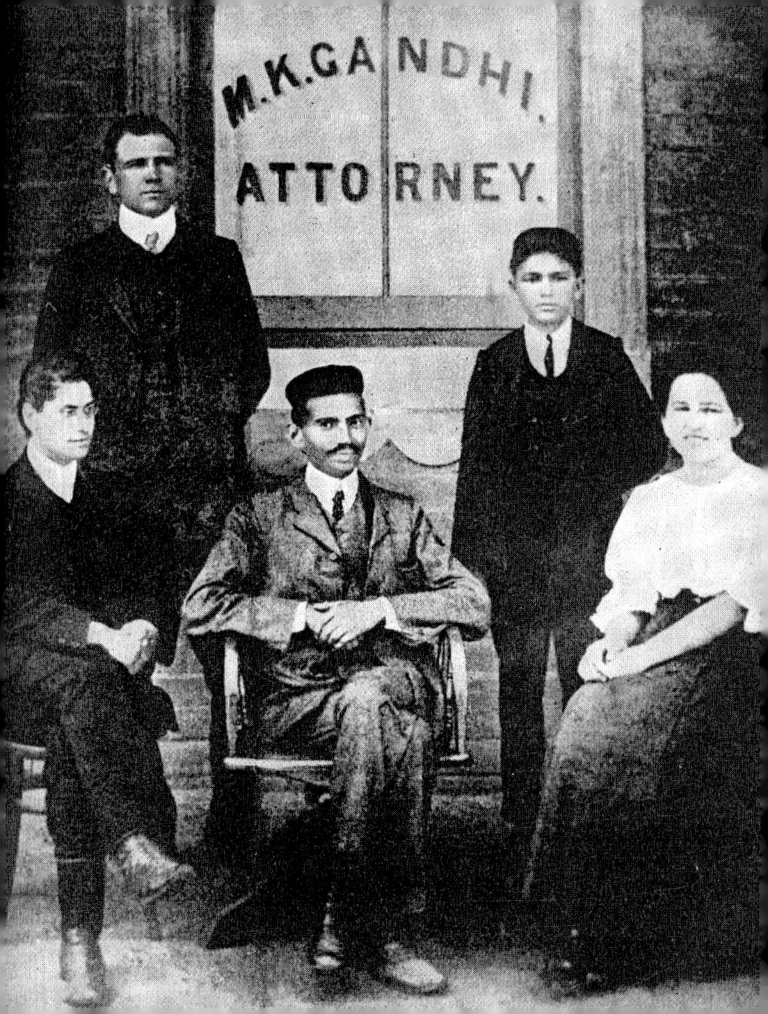
M.K.GANDHI.
ATTORNEY.

Gandhi with Sonja Schlesin and H.S.L. Polak in front of his office in Johannesburg, 1905.

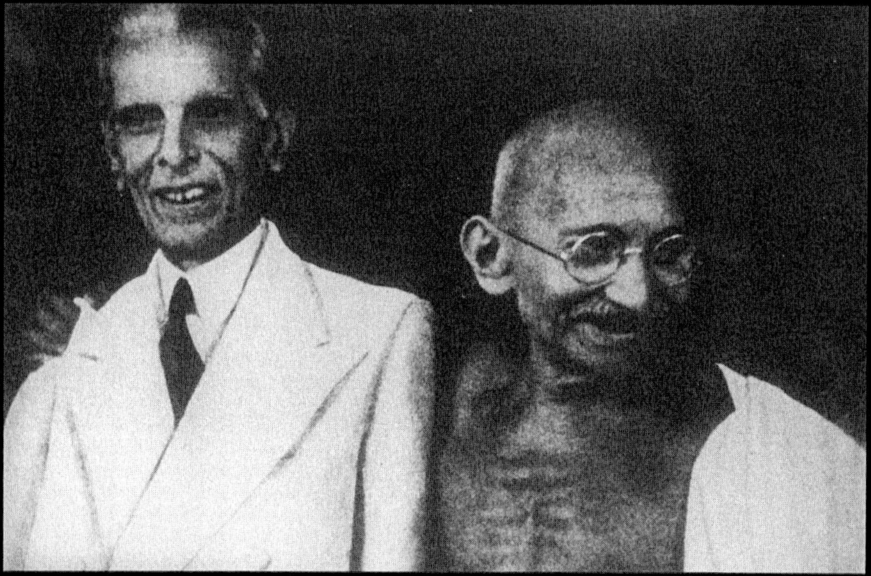

With M.A. Jinnah.

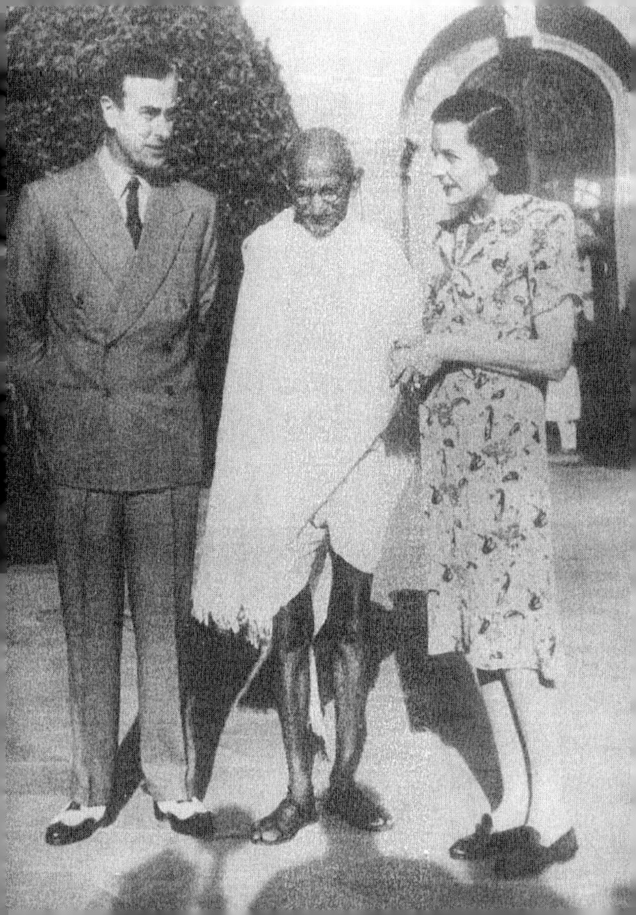

With Lord and Lady Mountbatten.

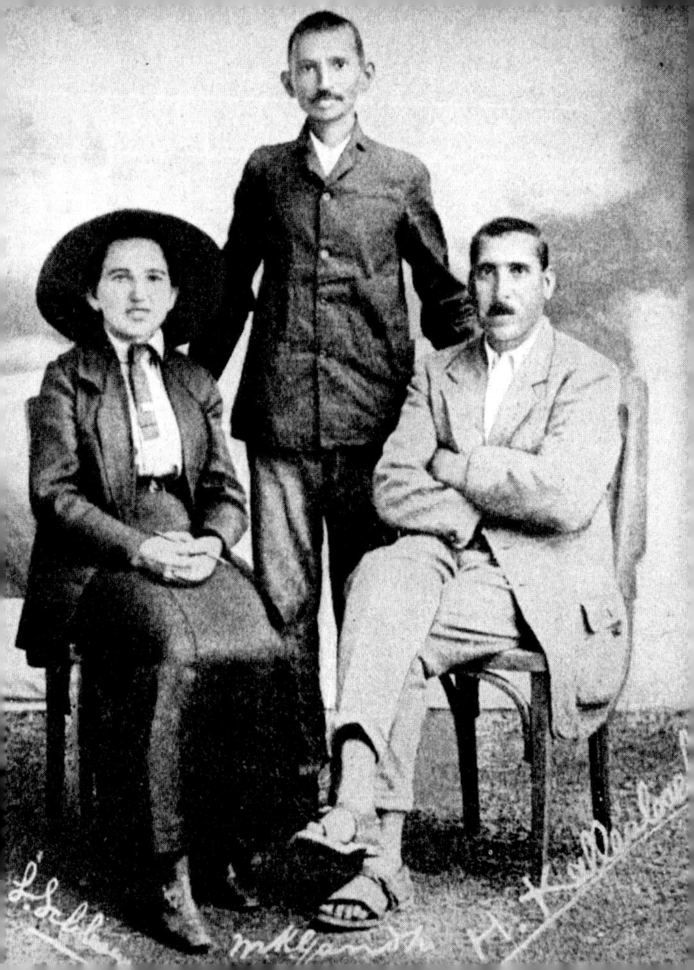

Gandhi with Hermann Kallenbach
and Sonja Schlesin, before the
Volkrust march, 1913.

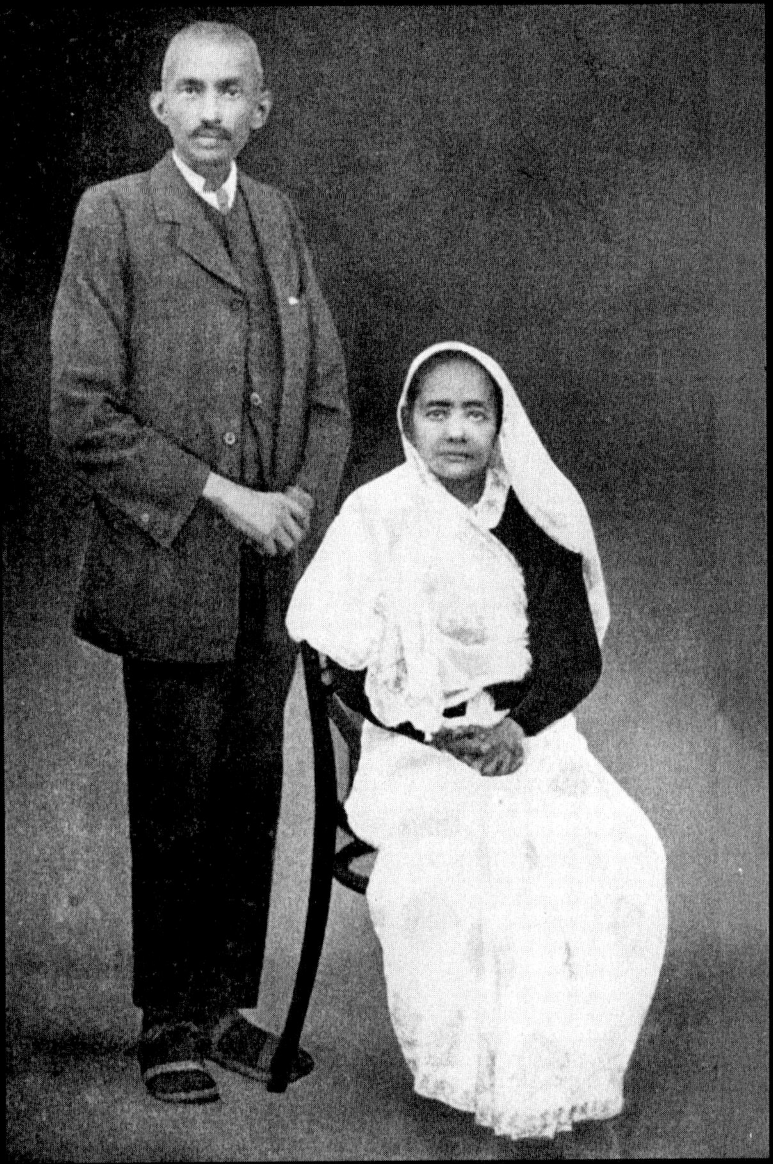

Gandhi and Kasturbai, Johannesburg, July 1914.

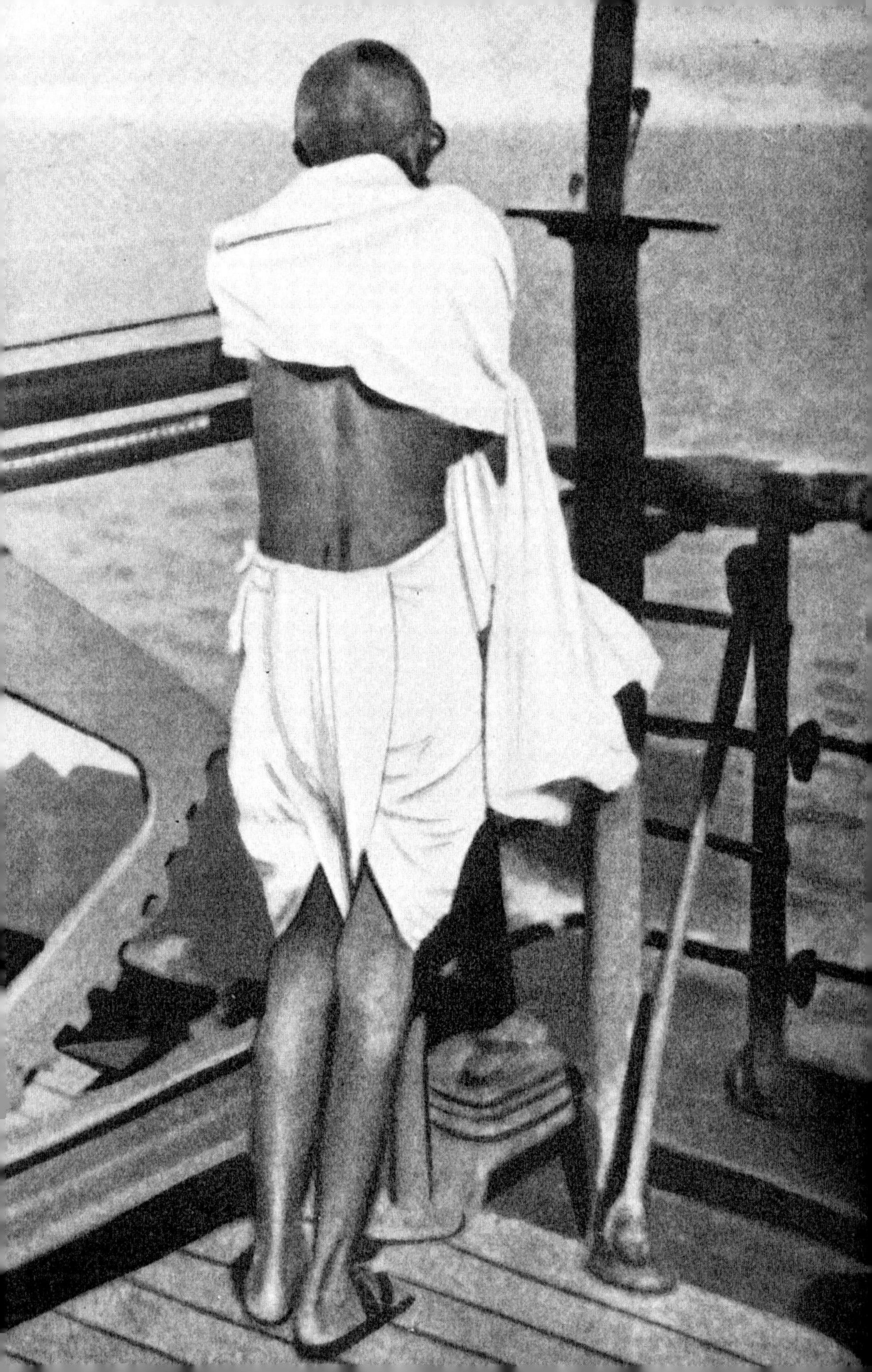

Away from India.

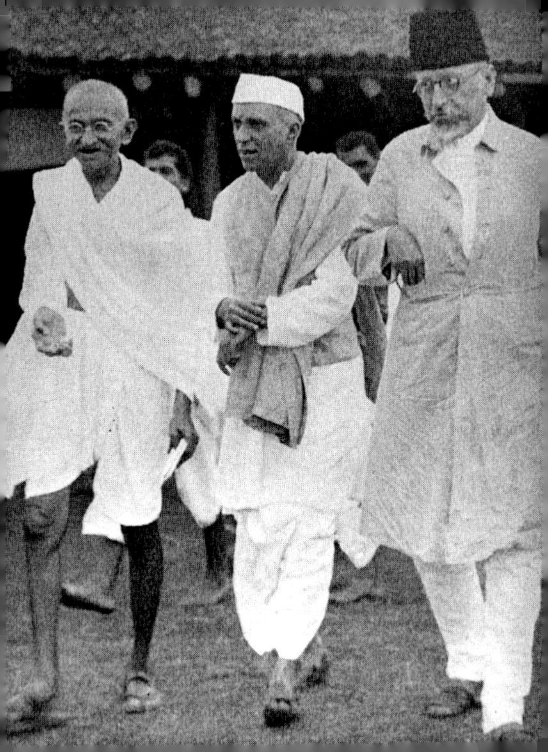

With Jawaharlal Nehru and
Maulana Azad.

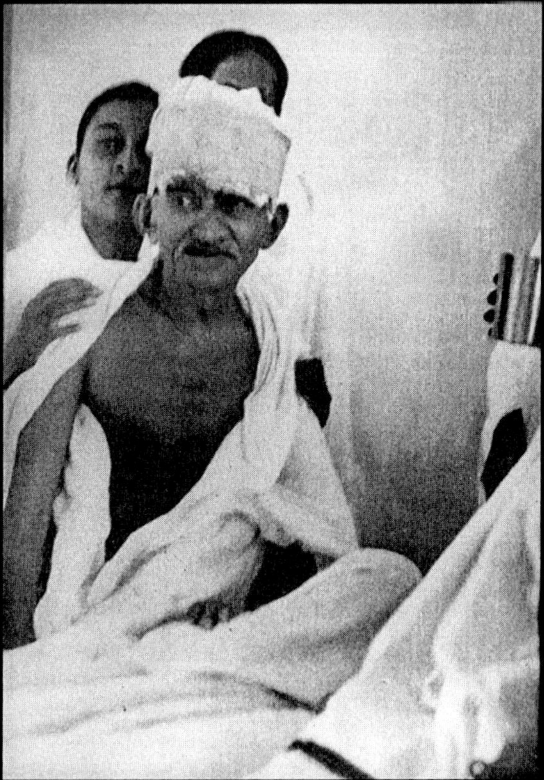

Gandhi breaking the fast, Rajkot, March 7, 1939.

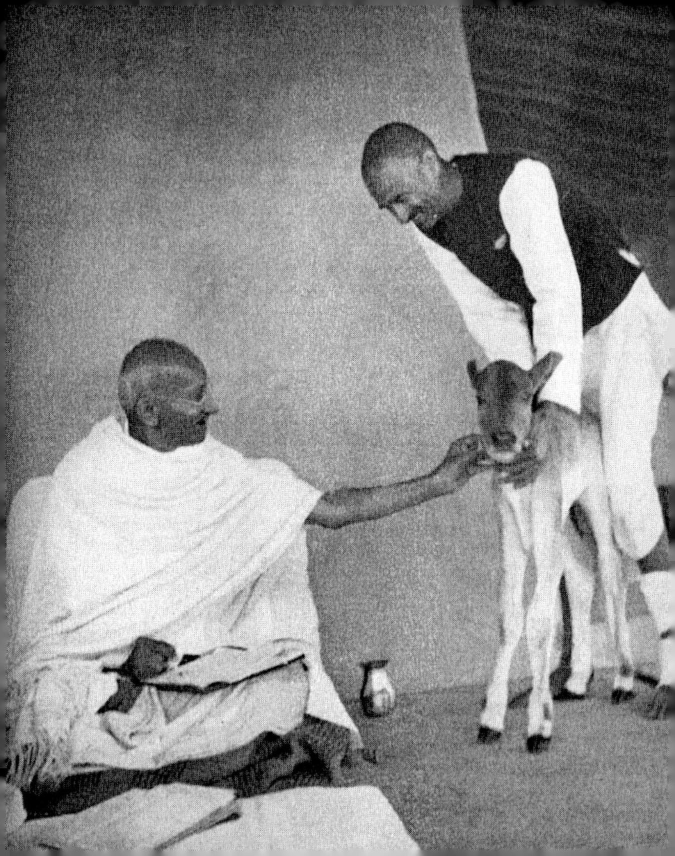

Gandhi and Balvantsinha patting a newborn calf, Segaon, September 1939.

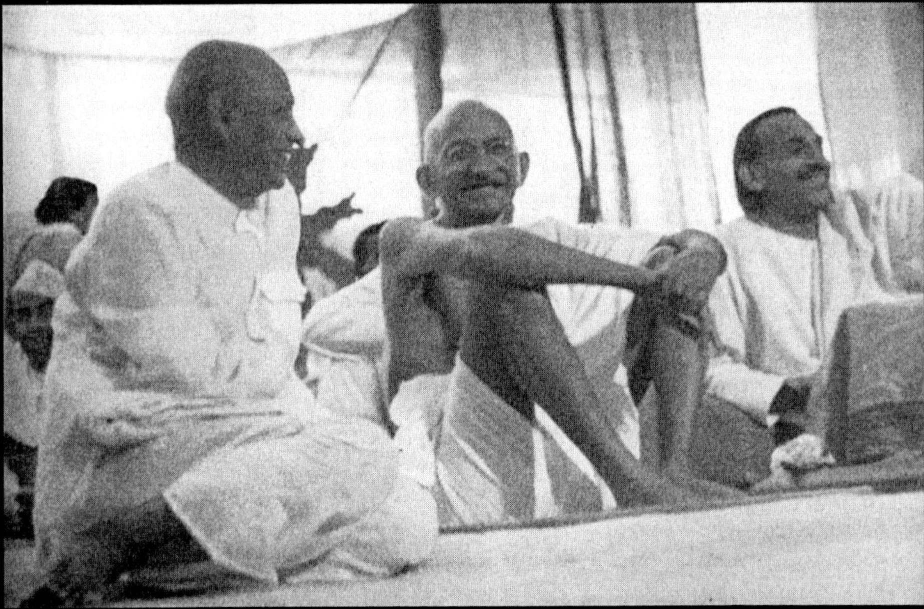

Ramgarh Congress, March 17, 1940.

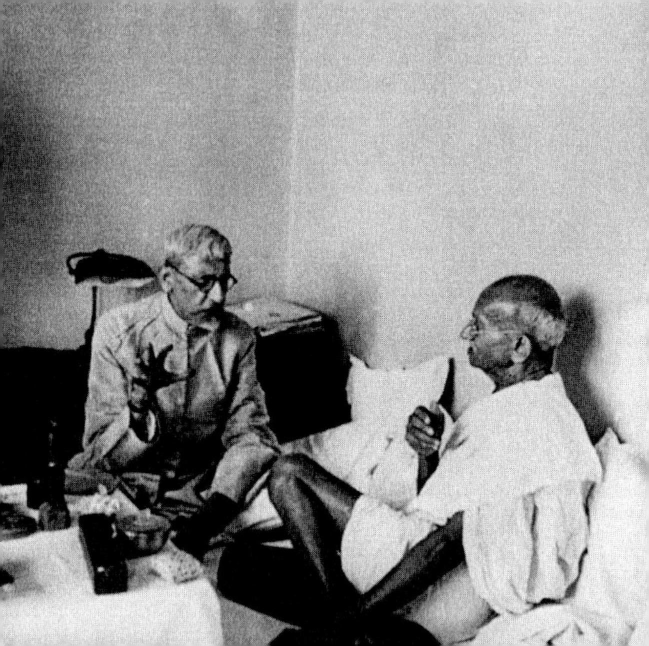

With Maulana Azad.

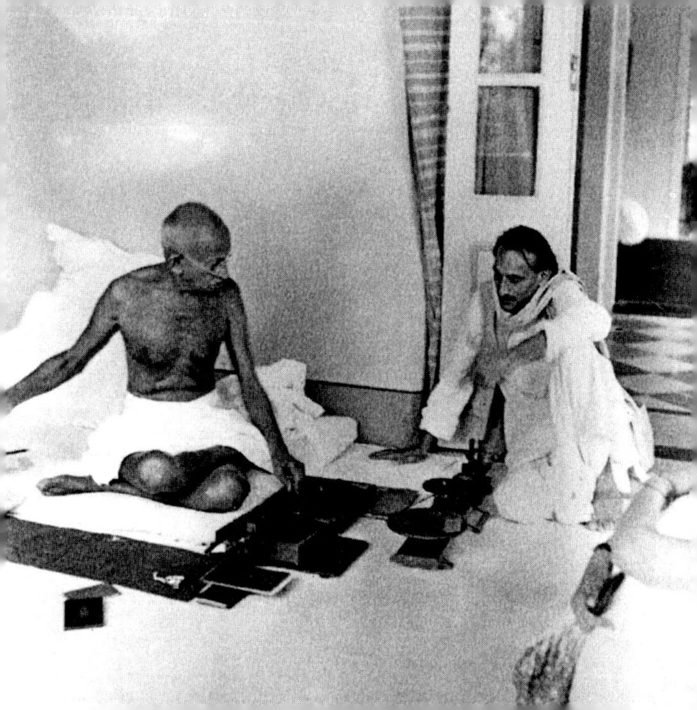

With Acharya Kripalani.

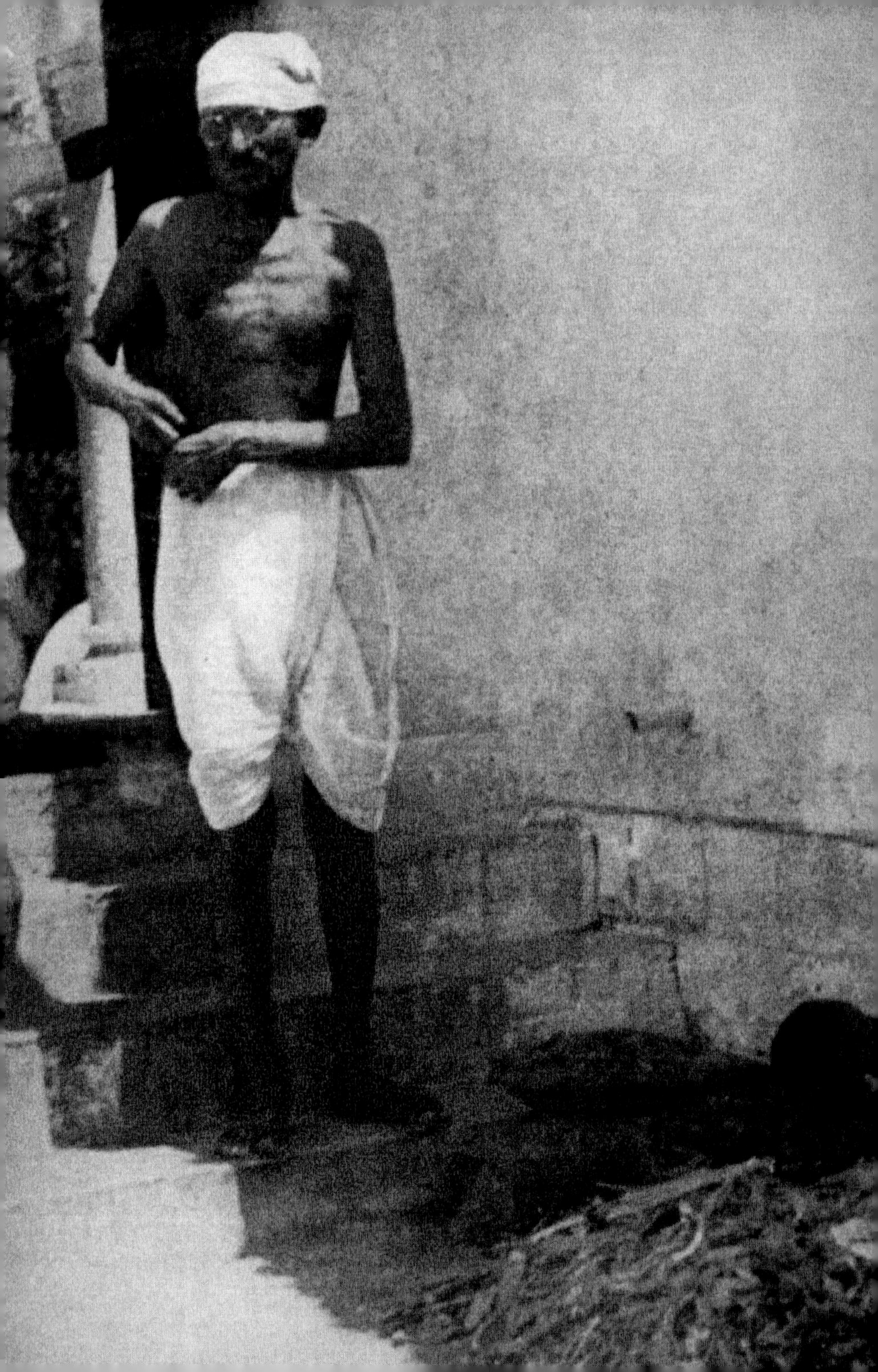

Gandhi getting ready for the
cleaning campaign, Wardha, 1936.

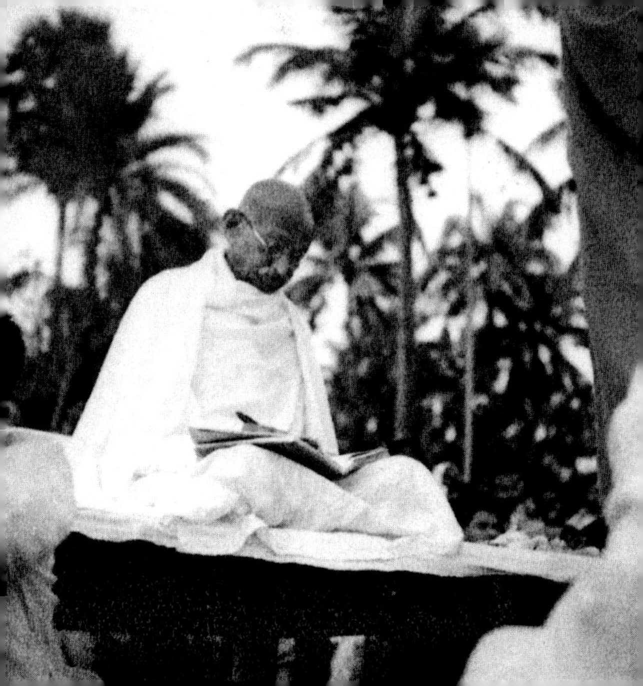

At prayer meet, Mumbai.

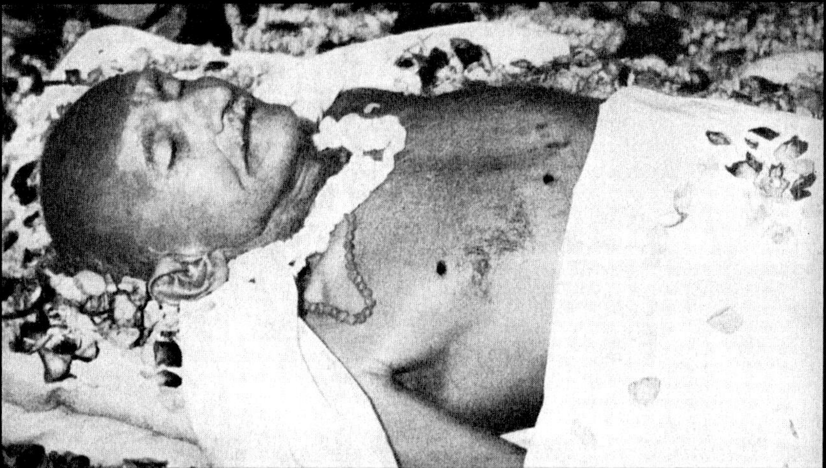

One with his Maker.

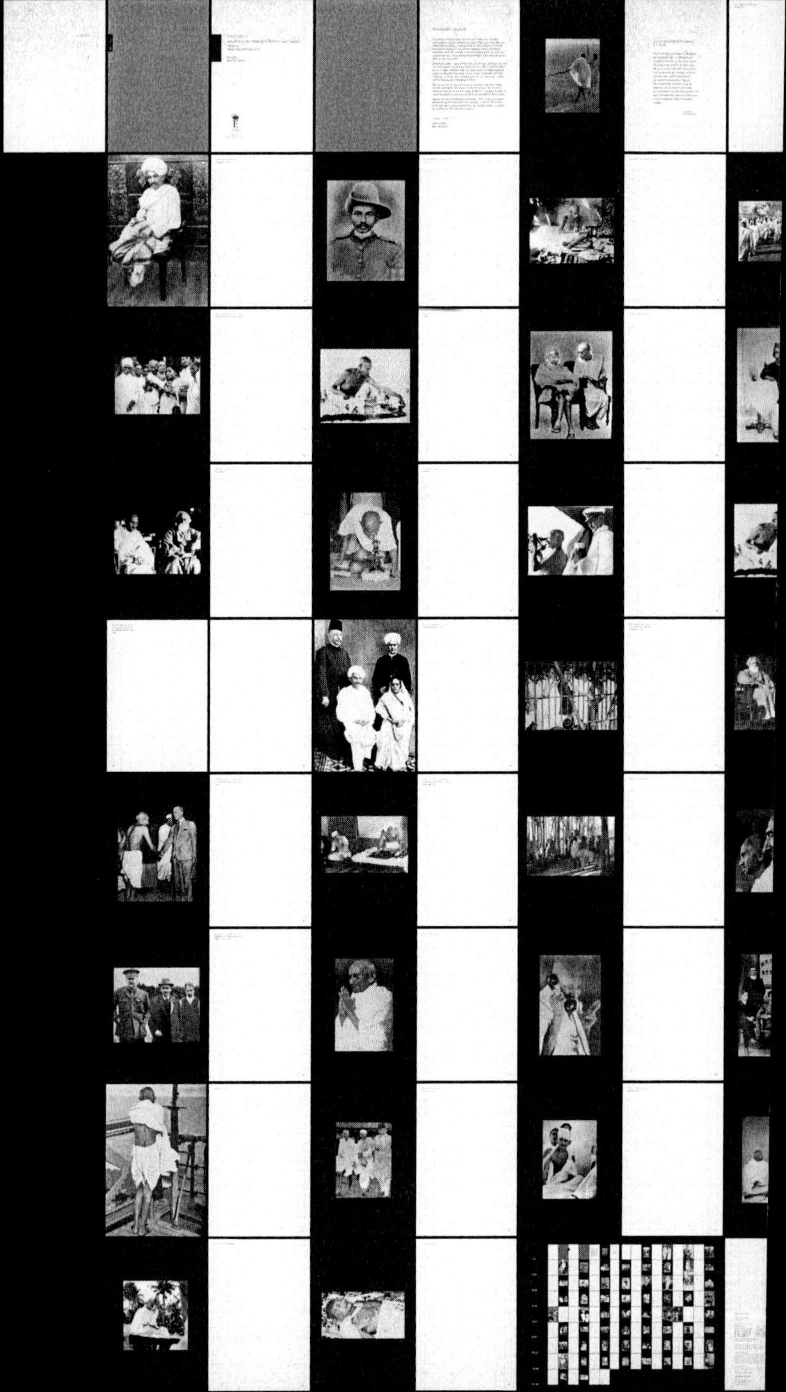

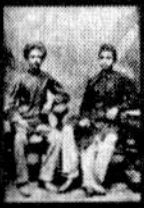
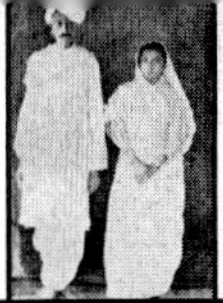
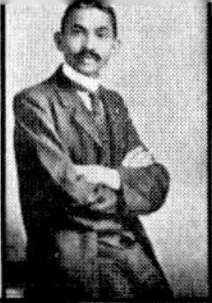
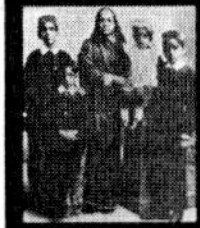
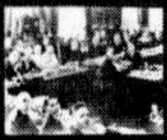
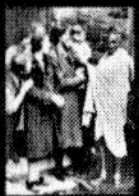
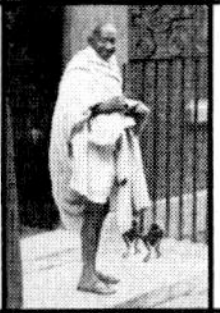
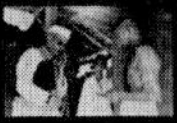
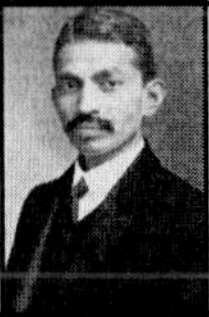
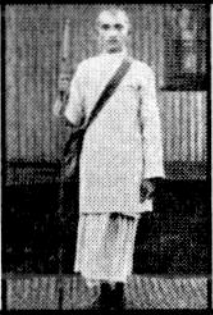
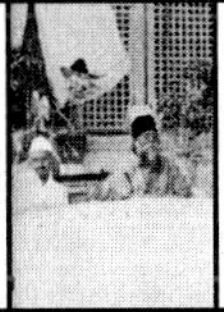
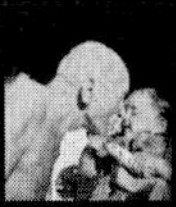
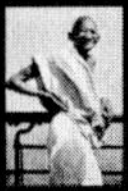
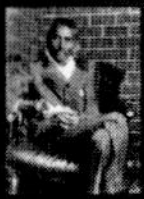
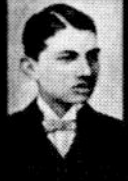
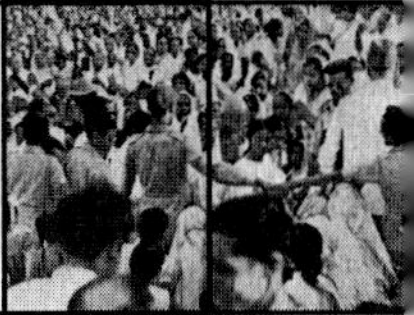
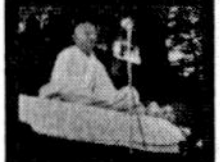
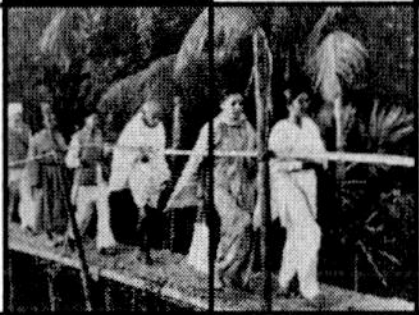
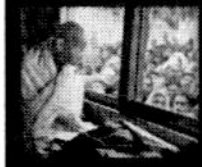
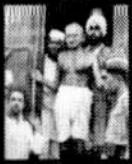
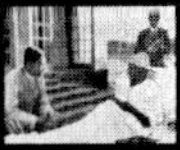
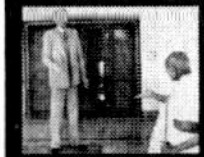
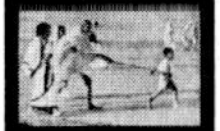
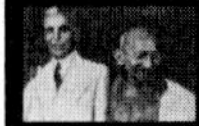
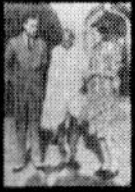
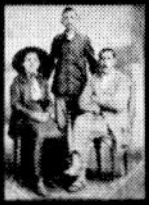
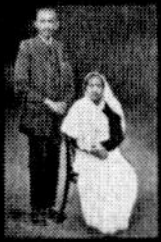
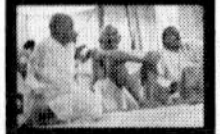
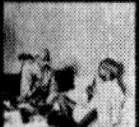
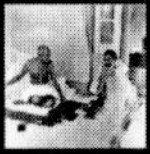
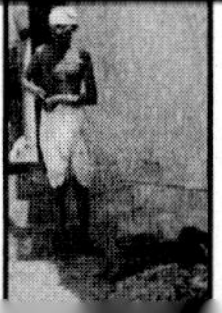

First published in 2015
by
LIMITED EDITIONS
an imprint of

ACADEMIC FOUNDATION

Delhi Sales Office:
4772-73/23 Bharat Ram Road,
(23 Ansari Road), Darya Ganj,
New Delhi - 110 002 (India).
Tel : +91-11-23245001 / 02.
Fax : +91-11-23245005.

Corporate Office:
No. 35, Sector 7,
IMT Manesar,
Gurgaon - 122050.
Haryana (India).
Tel: +91-124-4215070 / 71.

E-mail : books@academicfoundation.com
www.academicfoundation.org

Ageless India, Book 3
Apostle of the Twentieth Century—M.K. Gandhi:
Curated by Kinnari Bhatt and Tridip Surhud

Series Editor: Malvika Singh

ISBN 13: 9789332702035

Designed, printed and bound by
The Book Mint, New Delhi.
www.thebookmint.in